SELLING TO
SERVE

Sell Your Accounting & Bookkeeping Services

with Unshakeable Confidence

for More Than You Thought Possible

By James Ashford

3 5 7 9 10 8 6 4 2

First Published 2016

The Second Edition - The Revised & Updated Version - was published in 2021

Edited by Gillian French, Rachael Prideaux, Keith Lesser, Eleanor Shakeshaft, Mark Sweetman & The GoProposal Community

Acknowledgements

Every effort has been made to trace copyright holders. The publishers will be glad to rectify in future editions any errors or omissions brought to their attention.

Published by 'GoProposal Publishing', a trading style of GoProposal Limited. Registered in England with Company Registration No: 10004041. Registered Office: 16 Blackfriars Street, Salford, England, M3 5BQ

For more information visit www.GoProposal.com

*To my wife Bekki
and my children Lucy, Leo & Scarlett
without whom the updated version of this book
would have been completed 12 months earlier*

CONTENTS

Before We Begin 6

Foreword 7

Introduction 9

PART I - THE WHY

The One Problem 15

Who Is James Ashford? 43

The 7 Systems.. 63

Why Do We Systemise? 67

The Sales System.. 71

PART II - THE MINDSET

First Things First... 95

Why You *Really* Think Selling is Bad 97

9 Reasons You Struggle to Sell........................... 119

Why You Just Need to be You 143

4 Reasons Why Clients Really Say "No" 151

6 Common Objections to Your Services........... 169

Scope & Price.. 193

PART III - THE BLUEPRINT

The Effortless Sales System 215

Implement The System 269

Take Massive Action 270

The Red Pill 273

Remember… 279

What Our Members Say 279

A Note From The Author 283

A Favour 284

A Thank You 284

My Why 285

BEFORE WE BEGIN

As you go through this book, you're going to see me refer to accountants, accounting businesses and accounting services, but **you** may be a bookkeeper, or a CPA, a tax adviser, a payroll clerk, account manager, salesperson, partner, founder or CEO.

You may provide bookkeeping services, payroll services, tax services or advisory services.

Whoever you are and whatever you do, I'm so grateful that you've chosen to read this book and I don't want any of those words to get in the way of the message I have to share with you.

So please just switch out those words in your mind for whatever best describes you and what you do.

Because whatever the gift is that you have, I'm going to show you how to bring more of it to the world so you can make it even more impactful, profitable and rewarding.

Here we go.

FOREWORD

Occasionally you and I read great books. And very occasionally we see great movies. You're about to get into a really great book.

And let me ease you into it by referencing a great movie (at least I think it was great — particularly the music and its construction.)

The movie in question is The Greatest Showman. And there are several lines in the main musical theme that say it well:

> *It's everything you ever want,*
> *It's everything you ever need,*
> *And it's right here in front of you.*
> *This is where you want to be.*
> *It's everything you ever want,*
> *It's everything you ever need,*
> *And it's right here in front of you.*
> *This is the Greatest Show.*

James Ashford lives his Greatest Show every day and here he urges you and guides you to live yours too, with passion and belief.

Let's make it simple — a passionate belief that Accountants change lives AND that the Accounting BUSINESS is that …. a business. And like any business it's really all about people.

James' passion (and that belief) jumps out of every page of this book. It's like any great book — you feel that a) it's written just for you and b) the author is talking to you directly.

So, grab it with both hands AND as you do that, grab your highlighter too because it's for sure you'll highlight something on every page — idea after idea, insight after insight.

And as you do that, remember this: the power of any idea is only ever in its implementation.

So don't just highlight. Don't just commit. Actually do.

And here's why. Your Accounting Firm can be:

> *Everything you ever want,*
> *Everything you ever need,*
> *And it's right here in front of you.*
> *It really can be Your Greatest Show*

A show you share with people whose lives you change - every second, every day and in every way.

Go for it. You (and they) will be so glad you did.

Paul Dunn | Chairman | B1G1

INTRODUCTION

You're not running an accountancy firm; you're running a business.

But most accountants don't have a business, they have chaos.

And whenever you have chaos, you're unable to spend time on what's important and you'll be forever dragged into what's not.

You have clients taking up all of your time and energy, who don't pay you enough, want more and more from you and don't seem to value what you do, despite your best efforts.

You're constantly helping your team with the challenges *they* face, and everyone seems to have a different way of doing things, despite your attempts to systemise and bring in technology to get everyone working consistently.

And you're ultimately not getting the rewards from the hard work that you do, which include financial rewards, the gift of time, growth, joy and fulfilment, which is unfair and not why you started this.

You started in this industry because you wanted to impact your client's businesses and help them grow profitably and sustainably.

You wanted to use your skills and your innate abilities to serve others and to bring certainty and success into their lives.

But all of a sudden you find yourself running a business, leading a team and dealing with challenges you were never told about.

And then the game changed on you.

Cloud accounting came along which has simplified many things, but the software company's adverts imply that everything is now just a 'click of a button'. So, the work that you were doing, that was once highly valued by your clients, became less so, because they think *they* can now do it themselves.

But the service you provide is *still* complicated.

Your clients are *still* complex.

The nature of what you do *still* carries great risk.

So, while every other firm seems to be talking about all the great things they're doing, you still feel stuck, juggling clients, managing your team, working harder than ever and getting very little reward.

You feel frustrated and overwhelmed and wonder why every other firm seems to be smashing it out of the park.

Well, let me tell you... they're not; well at least not as many as would have you believe. But there are *some* firms who are.

Some firms *have* got their clients doing what *they* want them to do, in the way *they* want it doing, when *they* want it done.

These clients are paying two times, three times and even ten times more than they were before, AND they value the firm that serves them more than ever.

They have their staff all operating watertight systems in the way they should be run, consistently, whilst providing incredible value and experiences for their clients.

The owners of these firms feel more in control and are enjoying **increased energy, more time and more money**, so they can do more of what they love with the people they love.

I know that this is happening because I'm the Director of an accountancy firm myself, where I see it happening day in and day out. It's not that we're perfect by any means; perfect firms don't exist. We're work in progress. But we're proud of the many things that we do have right, which we willingly share, and these learnings and insights are now impacting thousands of other firms around the world.

But when you're in the thick of it yourself and you feel overwhelmed, it seems like there are 10,000 things to fix, it feels like you'll never solve them all and it's difficult to even know where to start.

As you try and solve one problem over here, another one erupts behind you, so you find yourself going round and round in circles.

This is because most of the problems people attempt to solve are *surface problems*. These surface problems are only symptoms of something much deeper; much more fundamental.

To solve the *real* problem, we have to go into the core of your business and fix the ONE problem that will make most of the 10,000 either disappear completely or become less relevant.

PART I
THE WHY

THE ONE PROBLEM

I have spoken to many accountants and bookkeepers who have hit rock bottom, where morale is at an all-time low and where they constantly question whether they're even good enough to do what they do.

I have spoken to firm owners in tears, who are fearful of how they're going to cover the payroll, whose marriages are on the rocks and who have no time for their kids. Seriously.

And when I speak to them about how they're trying to improve their situation, I nearly always discover that they're focussing on the wrong problems that only serve to take more of their time, more of their money and more of their energy.

It's tiring.

THE TWO CHALLENGES

So, there are two types of challenges that we face in our firms, two sets of problems to solve: **surface problems** and **core problems.**

Surface problems are obvious; core problems are not.

Surface problems attract people selling quick fix solutions, but who don't really know how to solve the fundamental, core problems.

Solving surface problems makes us feel good, but the results are nearly always short lived.

Surface problems are caused by core problems, so unless you address the core, surface problems will always persist.

Core problems always require a mind shift to solve, which means that YOU have to make a change.

Most people don't like to hear that, because they don't want to think that they might be the problem; they want to blame the world and attempt to change it. You can't.

I hear firms say, "It's those bad clients that cause all our problems. If I could just replace them with better clients, all our problems would be solved. Clients who really value us, pay us loads and do what we ask them."

But what if I told you that YOU'RE actually creating those bad clients and with one change, you could turn them great?

What if I told you that YOU have the power to do that, and you already have everything you need to turn everything around.

What if I told you that I've seen those 'bad clients' literally start paying 10 times more and become 'great clients' overnight.

You see, great clients don't just exist; they're not found... they're created.

Before we carry on, I must just caveat what I've just said with the fact that 'some' clients are total douchebags, always will be and need to be dropped. It's just far fewer than you currently think. If you want to know whether a client is bad or not, use our flowchart called *"Is this really a bad client?"* Grab it at **www.goproposal.com/bad** or scan the QR Code

So back to surface problems versus core problems.

Let me give you an analogy. So, let's say you have spots on your face and you believe this is the problem you need to solve. So, you're sold some pills and potions to solve the problem, only to find that they don't really work. Or they kind of do, but they also cause a new problem of headaches and the spots don't really go.

You then get new pills to solve the headaches and the side effects of those are spots (this actually happened to me when I was younger.)

This is because the real issue, the core issue, is that actually you need to change your diet, you need to get out into the sun more, you need to drink much more water, you need to exercise and they're the things that are actually going to get rid of the spots.

But all those things are fundamental shifts in psychology and behavior and therefore seem much harder to make, than buying some quick-fix, easy-to-pop pills.

And so, we come up with more elaborate methods of trying to cure the surface problems. We get even more extravagant potions and lotions and spend more on them.

But in actual fact, if you can just get under the skin of things and get to the core problem, we can prevent these surface problems from **ever** appearing again.

Rather than use analogies, let me actually show you what's going on in your accounting/bookkeeping/advisory business (delete as appropriate.)

THE CORE MODEL

I've developed a model to help you to understand visually what's really going on in your business, so you can better understand the problem you face and maybe even see it clearly for the first time.

I speak to a lot of accountants and bookkeepers, and I ask them why they do what they do; why did they go through all of their training, why did they set up a business and go through all of these hardships that they go through?

And the answer I repeatedly hear is that they want to positively **impact their client's business**, help them to have a more predictable business, a more profitable business, so they can have more wealth and security in their lives.

So that's the primary focus a lot of accounting firms have. They put their client's success first and this is very noble.

Their next goal is to build a **thriving culture**; to have a great team of people around them, who can run the systems and processes that they put into their business, who can evolve and grow and flourish and ultimately deliver this impact to their clients.

And then at some point in that discussion, fairly quietly, they will say that they're also doing this to **make money**.

So, they're the three goals of an accounting business:

- Impact clients
- Create a thriving culture
- Make money

But the first issue with this is the order. Very often they will put their *client's success* at the centre of everything.

But for me, you have to flip it around and put making money at the centre of your business for two, very important reasons.

IMPORTANT REASON #1

The first reason is, if you can't make money in your accounting business, you can't do any of the other things; you can't impact your clients, you can't invest in systems and processes, you can't afford to recruit, you can't afford to pay for the best team, you can't afford to train them and evolve them and you can't afford to attract the clients in the first place.

If money isn't at the centre of what you are doing, it causes all these other issues.

Now that's not to say that making money is your *reason why*; it doesn't have to be your purpose, your mission.

Your *reason why* is to serve your clients. That's beautiful. That's the thing that's going to get you out of bed in the morning and gets you excited about doing the work.

But the primary *function* of any business, has to be to make money, otherwise it eventually ceases to be.

IMPORTANT REASON #2

The other reason why it's so important for accounting businesses to get this right, is because that's what your clients are trying to do themselves.

So, if you can't do it for you, what chance have you got of helping your clients to do the same? This is not a selfish thing. It's the kindest thing you can do for your clients.

A financially healthy you, is a financially healthy them, but it starts with you.

And then if you're able to get this order right, maybe, just maybe you're able to achieve what we're all looking for in life - joy and fulfilment. This is the icing on the cake.

SURFACE PROBLEMS

There are however, things that make this idealistic model much more difficult to achieve. There are surface problems and core problems and it's the surface problems that distract you from seeing what's really going on at the core.

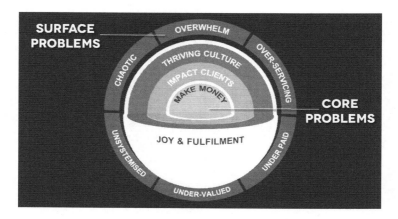

So, the first surface problem that we'll get is **over-servicing** clients. You're working too hard, working ridiculous hours and doing far more than you ever agreed you should.

There's a really dangerous word you've got to be careful of in the accounting industry, which is the word 'can'.

So, a client will ask you something, "*Can* you do this?"

And you say, "Yes, we *can* do that."

And it's in that one interaction where everything starts to go downhill, because what the client means is *can* you do it and *will* you do it?

And what you mean is, yes we *can* do it, *if* you pay for it. And it's somewhere in that confusion that you ended up doing more for your clients than they're actually paying for. But that's not the only reason you do that (more on that later.)

The second problem is that you're **underpaid** for the services that you're providing for your clients. Even if you didn't do more than you agreed, you're not getting paid enough in the first place. Most firms don't charge enough. They don't charge for everything, and if you're not getting paid enough, you expose yourself to huge risks.

The next problem this causes, ironically, is that you start to become **undervalued** by your clients. So, you'd think that if you do more for your clients and you don't charge them as much as you should, they would absolutely love you.

But the opposite is true. They actually start to undervalue what you do and when you start to scratch past the surface of that, it's because you're training them not to value what you do.

You give your time away from free. You give extra services away for free. And all the while you're inadvertently communicating to your clients that your services have no value, so guess what…. they stop valuing what you do.

The next issue is that you're not **systemised** (or at least not as well as you could be.)

As you start to grow your team, very often you allow them to do things the way they want to do them, because you're just grateful that you've got a member of staff to take on some of the workload. And that's fine initially, but then at some point, you realise that you don't have a business; you have a collection of individuals all doing things in their own way. This leaves you very vulnerable because if anyone were to ever leave, you're then exposed, and… everyone knows it.

Ideally you need systems running your business and then great people to operate those systems.

And if individual team members being in control of the business isn't bad enough, when you start to allow your clients to be in control of things as well, that's when we start to create real **chaos**.

This happens because someone has to be in charge of the relationship, and if it isn't you assuming that authority, it will be them, and mostly is.

When you put your clients in charge of the relationship; when you allow them to take control of everything, that's when we get to the final surface problem, which is **overwhelm**.

And overwhelm unchecked, can lead to real stresses and at the extreme end of that, depression, breakdowns and worse.

At this point the joy and fulfilment that we hoped to get from this business is unachievable and we're left with these surface problems which we do our very best to tackle.

But it's not the surface problems that are causing these issues at all. It's the fact that we've got a core problem, in the way the business fulfils its primary function - making money.

THE CORE PROBLEM

At the core of your accounting business is your **sales system**, and this is likely the root cause of your success or your problems.

Your sales system controls your ability to make money and forms the basis by which all client relationships are created.

If it isn't in balance and properly optimised, then you will be losing money, losing time, losing energy, losing control of clients, control of staff and control of all other areas of your business and you will be suffering with a great deal of frustration, overwhelm and ultimately chaos.

Are you experiencing any of these?

If so, firstly, it's not your fault. They trained you in how to become skilled in your craft, but they didn't train you in how to then sell your services to clients in a mutually beneficial way. Why? Because they don't know either.

Secondly, I can help you to solve this problem.

I've been helping thousands of firms around the world who have been courageous enough to acknowledge that the world of accounting has changed; accountants and bookkeepers who joined the profession, through wanting to provide value and who are sick of it being reduced to a necessity; those who have had enough of putting up with crap from clients, and not getting paid enough for a service that's so challenging to deliver and fraught with risk.

Those firms who want to give more value to their clients AND have them appreciating that value.

Those who want to get paid more for the hard work that they do, so they can build a more profitable accounting business.

Those who want to have the option to work less or on higher value activities so they can feel more joy and fulfilment.

Each time I have taken firms on that journey, regardless of what they believe their immediate challenge to be, it nearly **always** starts in the same place... with the sales system.

The sales system ultimately controls your profitability, and if you can't control that, it's almost impossible to control anything else.

Making your sales system work will require you to have a certain mindset, certain processes and certain tools to achieve success, which we will go through within the pages of this book.

Your sales system is the key to unlocking the value for your firm and the value for your clients.

Put simply, the sales system consists of two elements; the **scope** of work that you agree with the client, in exchange for the **price** they're going to pay for it.

So long as that value exchange is fair, in balance and optimised, you (should) make money.

The only thing that makes this system work is '**selling.**'

Without a sale, no value can be exchanged, and this is the first point in this book where you feel uncomfortable, right?

You've been with me so far and may have even felt like I'm a mind reader with what I have been describing. You were really by my side, enjoying the journey, nodding along and looking forward to seeing where it goes, then BOOM…

…with that one word, you felt something deeply uncomfortable in the pit of your stomach… **selling.** Urgh!

A part of your brain just touched the brakes as you considered what's ahead and whether you want to even go there or not.

This is because we've just hit a conflicting thought in your mind: You want to give value, but you don't want to sell (or at least you don't want to be *seen* to be selling.)

Am I right?

The psychology that controls this feeling is fascinating and so deep. I don't want you to worry about that feeling for now, just park it and know that I've got you. I know it's there. I also know *why* it's there and throughout this book, I promise I will help you to come to understand that feeling in a way you never have before, and I WILL help you to remove the conflict.

So, hold that thought and let's go back into the core.

The core is where the problem starts. It's where we typically get the scope wrong for a number of reasons.

You probably don't have a clear methodology for defining the scope of work.

If you do, it's probably not specific enough.

If it is, it's probably not clearly communicated to everyone involved in that client relationship, from your side and theirs.

And if it can be, you probably still agreed to do more than you're getting paid for, because you want to 'help them' right? (FYI, that's not the real reason you agreed to do more than they're paying for. More on that later too.)

You agree to do more and so, RIGHT AT THE START OF THE RELATIONSHIP... IN ITS MOST FORMATIVE PERIOD.... the scope was out of balance with the price... BEFORE YOU EVEN STARTED WORKING WITH THEM! What chance did that relationship have?

And over time, as more people get involved in that relationship, as the client makes more demands, because of a lack of systems, avoidable bottlenecks and a fatally flawed psychology, the scope grows more and more out of balance.

The worst I've ever seen is for this scope to have grown for seven years, totally unchecked, taking the firm to the brink of disaster.

Just look at this visual representation of an out of balance sales system. Do you think that is a fair representation of some or all of your client relationships?

Do you feel that this is something you **must** solve? Because only when it's a MUST, will you take the required actions needed to make the change.

If so, let's get clearer on the two main components.

SCOPE

Scoping is hard.

The scope is the detailed promise of the value you're going to provide to your clients.

However, accounting & bookkeeping services are complicated.

You have different combinations and different levels of service that you provide to your clients.

And to compound this problem, businesses are complex.

There are so many factors that the business brings to the equation, such as their revenue, how many staff they've got, how many transactions they have and the quality of their record keeping, to name just a few.

Even if it's an individual you're acting for, they can have different levels of complexity with income streams, pension funds, child support and properties.

And normally, the knowledge for how to effectively scope a client, sits in the heads of only a few people, not in the hands of the people who are in the best position to know what's really going on.

Then what starts out wrong, gets worse over time because the scope is rarely recalibrated and if it is, it's normally only done once a year, which is probably not often enough.

Another key challenge is how long scoping takes to do properly. This is not just because you've got to go through all the services and the service levels, but you must ensure that you cover yourself from a risk point of view through the generation of an accurate and all-encompassing engagement letter.

If you do additional work that's not covered in the engagement letter, not only are you not getting paid for it, but you are exposing yourself to great risk if something were to go wrong.

That's called a lose-lose.

But let's say you're really good at scoping, you have a systemised approach and you're able to complete it within, let's say two hours. When do you have two hours free? Today? This week?

So, it could actually take you until next week just to find those two hours to complete the task. It's one of those important things, but never seems urgent, and because it takes that time, most people delay doing it and it only gets worse.

The worse it gets, the less likely we want to do it because of the pain associated with telling the client their fees are going up, so what do we do... delay it some more.

This would make you laugh if it didn't have such painful consequences.

And here's the other issue that we face as an industry... accounting services are intangible.

As a client, I don't get to feel anything.

If I go and buy a car today, I get to sit in it. I get to smell the leather seats. I get to feel the steering wheel. I get to put my foot down and accelerate and move the thing forward. I get to feel this physical thing.

If someone is coming in and signing up for your services, over the next 10 years, if they're paying the correct fee, *it's the equivalent of buying a car.*

They're paying the same amount as they would be for a car, but they don't get anything physical.

You provide this magical, mythical service.

The client gives you some information and magically their staff get paid or a tax return gets filed or their debtor days get reduced or whatever, but they don't get to hold or feel anything.

And so what you must become an expert at, is communicating the value of what you provide to your clients, by providing well-articulated scopes, presented within professional proposals. This gives it a certain physicality and sense of certainty.

You have to make the intangible, tangible if it has any chance of being understood and valued.

PRICE

The other half of the sales system is **price.**

Typically, firms are not consistent in the way that they price. They don't charge the same fees across all services, across all of their clients or across all different team members or partners. It also varies between historic clients, current clients, discount-asking clients,

clients who are 'friends', clients who were referred by friends and clients whose kids go to the same school as yours.

So that lack of consistency really starts to cause some major problems.

As with scoping, the knowledge for how to price properly exists in a few people's heads, typically the partners or the senior people within the business. These tend to be the busiest people in the business, so they also become the bottleneck.

So, if you're trying to establish the correct price, this probably has to be extracted from the people who have the least time to figure it out, which leads to one of two actions; either they'll just come up with a finger in the air price, or they'll base the price on a similar client, who is most likely underpaying you as well.

This method relies entirely on luck and the price given will either lose you money, enable you to break even or make a profit. Just roll the dice and choose.

Instead, you need a consistent, systemised and profitable approach to pricing that everyone can use with **every client**, every time.

Oooh! What did that voice in your head just say? Was it something to the effect of "That won't work! I have some clients who would never pay the same as others, and in fact, I wouldn't be comfortable charging more anyway."

If so, that was another conflicting belief rearing its head - I want to be more profitable in my firm (but not with every client.)

Interesting.

Anyway... the reason you need a consistent pricing system is because you need something that can be improved. You see, pricing is never solved, it's only ever tuned. It's never perfected, only ever improved. But you need something concrete in the first place to improve, otherwise it will never get any better. **Version one is better than version none!**

Pricing is a movable feast.

You need to be constantly looking back at it and figuring out what is the challenge here. Why isn't this client profitable? Why are we now not getting paid enough for this service? Is it a service issue? Is it a member of staff issue? Is it this type of client? Is it the industry that we're serving? What are the factors that are making us out of whack with this price?

You need to be able to take that knowledge and feed it back into a system so it's always getting better. It will never be perfect. You need to accept that, but you need a method of constantly evolving it and improving it otherwise IT WILL GET WORSE. Nothing stays the same.

GETTING BALANCE

So, the first goal is to restore **balance** within the sales system by bringing the scope and price into alignment. This makes it a fair exchange of value for what you're providing and what you're getting in return.

This occurs when confusion is removed around scoping and replaced with sophistication. Regardless of how complicated a service is and however many factors there are that could contribute to that complexity, there's always a way; always an appropriate level of logic that can be applied.

On the other side, you need a consistent, clear and logical pricing framework that's accessible for everyone to use.

Once you have those two elements, balance is restored.

The next thing is to **optimise** what you already have i.e., make the scope greater and make the price greater.

I'm a big believer that you're already in possession of everything you're looking for, so optimising is about giving more value to the clients you already have.

You do this by having better conversations that unlock what their real problems are and creates opportunities for you to solve them.

Your value in the world is directly proportional to the size of the problems that you can solve, so if you can solve bigger problems for your clients, you can be more valuable.

Once you've restored balance and optimised what you already have, you then need to **repeat** this process at appropriate intervals, to keep them in balance.

In our firm we apply the **1-3-12 Rule**. This is where we review payroll services with every client every **1-month**, bookkeeping services every **3 months,** and all other services every **12 months**.

This keeps the core in balance and confirms why the ability to effectively scope and price using a consistent sales system needs to be accessible by everyone, because if it's not, the bottlenecks will prevent this from ever happening.

This ultimately maximises the money-making potential of your business, with a healthy sales system at its core.

At this point, many, if not all of the surface problems either drop away or become less relevant and you can start to come back to feeling joyful and fulfilled, which is why you started out doing what you're doing in the first place.

If the core is out of balance, you will be expelling large amounts of energy trying to solve unsolvable surface problems and feeling no sense of joy or fulfilment. This is tiring and not possible to maintain.

But when the core is in balance, the surface problems drop away, you start to feel joy and fulfilment and are energised to grow your business which leads to even more joy and more energy.

This is what I want for you.

This is how I want your firm to look and feel.

This is the breakthrough I want to help you to make, and there's one curious thing about breakthroughs.

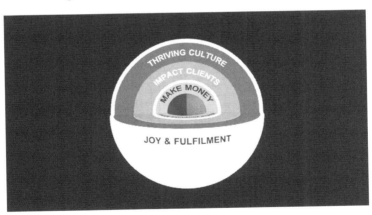

MAKING THE BREAKTHROUGH

Breakthroughs are **instant** events.

Preparing to make the breakthrough, figuring out the reasons *why* you *must* make this breakthrough, harnessing the correct *mindset* for the breakthrough, finding the right people to help you to make the breakthrough and acquiring the *roadmap* to make the breakthrough is what takes the time.

But the actual breakthrough moment is instant.

I've seen a struggling firm owner go from not being able to pay her staff, to increasing her highest client's fee **by ten times,** within two days.

But this wasn't the first time she attempted to make the breakthrough. The first time was six months prior, where she'd attempted to setup a new pricing system and get clients on the phone to reprice them. She'd tried for weeks but failed to make the breakthrough. Why? Because at that time, it wasn't a **must.**

The pain of asking a client for more money, in her mind, was more painful than her lack of ability to generate any profit.

As humans, we are hard-wired to move away from pain, and faced with two pains, we'll move away from the greatest one.

Over the course of the next six months, her own financial situation deteriorated and all of a sudden, the pain of what she faced in her own bank account became greater than the prospect of having a hard conversation with her clients.

She reached back out to us, we grabbed her by the hand, put her through our fast-track process and within two days... her breakthrough.

What had changed in that time? Our process was exactly the same as the first time she came to us. What had changed, was that it had now become a **must** for her.

A must is when you say, "No more. We cannot carry on like this anymore. This must change. We must do this instead. We must do this now."

THAT'S when you have the ability to run through walls. THAT'S when breakthroughs happen.

How long does it take to quit smoking?

I smoked for nearly 15 years and knew it was wrong and wanted to stop. I tried hypnotherapy, psychotherapy, patches, self-education, everything. Why did nothing work? Because I associated more pain with stopping than I did with carrying on. We're very simple creatures at the end of the day; we move away from the greatest pain. That is encoded into our reptilian brain – can it eat me?

Then one day I went to see a brilliant man called Tony Robbins. He pointed out what would happen if I continued on this path. And as I took this course of action forward in my mind, the pain built and built until it became mentally unbearable.

At that point the balance tipped. It was no longer a choice; it was a must. At that point I associated more pain with *continuing* than with *stopping*, so I stopped, just like that and have never smoked since.

But I had to have been prepared mentally to make the breakthrough. It's better to be prepared for an opportunity and it not arrive, than for it to arrive and not be prepared.

So how long does it take to quit smoking? Instantly!

But know this... when you make the breakthrough, **80% is having the mindset** and **20% is having the map**, so you must be prepared to challenge your thinking, because the thinking that has got you to where you are now, is not going to get you to where you really want to be.

So, let's recap...

You are not running an accountancy firm; you're running a **business.**

Most accountants don't have a business, they have chaos.

And while you have chaos, you're unable to spend time on what's important and you'll forever be dragged into what's not.

You need a business, which runs on systems, and then you need your team to run the systems.

The first system an accounting business needs to implement and have watertight, in balance and fully optimised, is the sales system. Why? Because this is where you...

- Make your money
- Define the value you're going to provide to your client in exchange for the money they're going to pay you
- Take complete control of the client relationship and get them behaving as you want them to from the start
- Demonstrate that you are the expert on how to build a profitable business
- Remove the chaos, the frustration and the feeling of overwhelm once and for all

At the end of the day, you are a business, and the primary function of a business is to make money.

The only two ways you can make money is to get more clients or give more value to the clients that you already have.

The only way you can do either of those things, is by selling your services to them.

And you can only sell your services if you have a successfully implemented sales system that can be used across your business.

Are you on board with this?

Are you ready to go on a deep journey with me? A journey into some dark areas of your mind that you've never shone a light on before. A journey that will challenge some of your most limiting beliefs, remove your conflicting thoughts, reveal the blueprint for a successful sales system and give you the unstoppable confidence to do what you now perceive to be hard, in order to make life so much easier?

Are you ready for **your** breakthrough?

Yes?

Great, but why should you listen to me?

WHO IS JAMES ASHFORD?

Before we really get stuck into this, I want to tell you a little bit about myself, so you can understand where I'm coming from and why.

I've always had a passion for business, which comes from a deep interest and belief in people who want to do good in the world.

Business is a great way to do good, by positively impacting the people you give employment to, the people you serve and the products and services you bring to the world.

Since the age of 15 I have always been entrepreneurial, starting many mini business ventures, some of which made some money, but most of which failed.

I studied product design to master's degree level and went on to work in many varied roles from being a landscape designer, to teaching art in prisons, a close-up magician and working in sales.

I found that being a close-up magician made me a good salesperson, because I was able to go to table after table of normally quite drunk people, who typically hated magicians, didn't believe in magic and didn't want me there, interrupting their enjoyable night. I had 5 minutes to sell them on the idea that magic was real, which I did, again and again.

At weddings, there is always the one table, normally the couple's friends from school, who are sat the farthest away from everyone else. They tend to be the rowdiest and there is a code amongst magicians, which is to leave that table until the end and try to sneak away without having to go to them, saying you ran out of time.

I had a different view; leave that table until the end, make them think I was deliberately avoiding them, but secretly I knew they were the table to conquer and I was already prepared.

You see, two weeks prior to the wedding I'd already asked the bride which this table was going to be, and in fact, who was going to be the worst person on this table AND what was their phone number. Before everyone sat down, I marked exactly where this person was sitting and had the best trick planned for them.

MY code was, win that table over and I win over the room.

In 2008, working in a sales role and with a baby on the way, the recession hit, and I was made redundant from two companies in very quick succession.

So, believing I could do better and wanting to be in control of the money I made, I set up my first 'proper' business, which was a web design and marketing agency.

I did that so that I could give my family the life I wanted for them and for us to have more time together.

Spoiler alert, it didn't work out like that at all.

I set up the agency and realised very quickly that I had no idea how to run a business and needed to learn fast.

I was told to read a book called eMyth Revisited and began learning about systems. And while I knew about them theoretically, implementing them in a way that they stuck, so that everyone did what they were meant to do, every single time, to a high standard, was another thing altogether.

But I found that I had a great testing ground through the clients I worked with, because not only were we able to help them with their marketing, but we were also able to implement sales and marketing systems into *their* businesses.

This made us very unique as we weren't just creating websites, but we were then actively impacting the sales systems within those organisations.

We were successful on a small scale and profitable for a time, but in the end, that business failed.

It failed because I didn't have the full finance function in place in that business.

We ended up making a series of small financial decisions, each taking us one degree off course which, compounded, over time and left unchecked, took us to the edge and I didn't even know.

I was acting on historical financial data that was given to me several months after the year end.

We chose to invest a large amount of resources into a start-up business idea that one of our clients brought to us, which showed promise. Rather than take any money, we saw it as an investment and took a 50% shareholding instead. This would have represented a significant fee for us, but instead represented a large loss of time that led to no financial reward.

We brought on a handful of larger projects who wanted to pay over 12 months rather than up-front. These ground our cashflow down to a halt, because we were effectively funding their projects for them.

I received a large personal tax rebate. We couldn't believe our luck and it was a welcomed break from the financial challenges of paying myself a low wage for so long. We splashed out on a handful of things and went on holiday.

When I returned, there was a brown envelope on the doormat saying that we owed several thousand pounds in unpaid tax for the business. I recognised the amount instantly. My heart stopped.

The tax we thought we were paying for the business had been paid into my personal tax account by mistake, which is why it looked like a tax rebate. We had to find the money and pay it back.

We managed the VAT filing ourselves and missed a deadline, which then triggered a very lengthy and time-consuming inspection, trawling through endless receipts and invoices for days. It uncovered errors in our filing and small businesses don't have days to devote to non-revenue generating tasks.

We had a strong process for clearly communicating prices to clients and signing them up instantly, but the prices in the system were too low.

We never had anything like monthly management accounts or budgets or forecasts. I never had anything I could use to make decisions other than a hunch about things and ultimately, those hunches proved wrong, which was a real shame because we did have a lot right too.

I remember proudly bringing in a potential business partner and when he showed me under the bonnet of what was *really* going on, it was like a blindfold had been removed from my eyes. I could see for the first time that we were on the edge of a cliff, about to go over. I felt sick.

In a bid to backpedal as fast as we could, we instantly tripled all of our prices.

I went into a proposal meeting two days later, nervous about presenting a potential project fee of £15k, which would have been £5k just a few days earlier.

The client signed up on the spot.

Rather than be excited, I was gutted.

I reflected on how I'd been underselling our services for all those years. I was gutted about how we'd extended credit to clients or effectively given our services away for free, under the guise of 'investing.' I was gutted at my lack of financial acumen and how I'd allowed our accountant to convince me that "Management Accounts were overkill for a business of our size."

We had cloud accounting software in place, but this gave us a false sense of security. Just because we had the technology, didn't mean we had the financial maturity or necessary skills to run a robust finance function.

We had no rainy-day fund; no emergency cash set to one side.

We never reviewed our overheads or looked at ways of reducing them.

We had no budget or cash flow forecast.

Tax bills and our annual accounting bill always came as a surprise.

We lived hand to mouth.

But when you start out in business, you don't know what you don't know. You're an expert in your craft but you don't just get given the required skills to install a finance function required to make the business work. You have blind spots to this, which if someone doesn't point out to you, will cause a collision further down the road.

This is why you need trusted people around you who recognise those, who are prepared to have the difficult conversations with you and tell you what you need, not just what you think you want.

As a business owner you think *great, I have an accountant and pay him what seems like a lot of money, so everything must be ok. We have some cool looking accounting tech and paying tax bills and running payroll seems easy enough. What can go wrong?*

Remember, small financial decisions that each take you one degree off-course, left unchecked, compounded, over time, will take you to the edge.

All of these financial stresses had led to some staffing challenges. I was working harder than ever IN the business by that time, so, feeling beaten, and with a loss of enthusiasm for what we were doing, I folded the business.

I know what it's like to sit in front of my staff and say "You know that business you've been helping me to build for the last 4 years. It's gone. It's over. Go home."

I know what it's like to go back to my wife and say "You know all those late nights I worked and things I missed out on because of that business I'd been growing? It's over. I've messed up. We need to remortgage the house." (I had been advised to take a loan out to buy a car, which I'd personally guaranteed.)

I know the sense of shame and feeling that I'd let down my clients and suppliers who'd backed us.

And I also know what it's like to dust myself off, pick up the pieces and start again with a renewed sense of enthusiasm for what I knew I must do.

I asked myself the question… what would I do if I knew I could never be paid for it?

And it was to work with businesses; to light up business owners and help them to make that breakthrough towards what was possible for them.

So, I went to work, studying business strategies from some of the world's leading experts, who were setting businesses on paths towards exponential growth within very short time frames.

I travelled to the US and studied business systematisation from those who I considered to be the very best at creating repeatable processes, which led to incredible client experiences.

I learnt about ethical selling and the psychology about the real reasons people feel compelled to do so much work for free, and why they don't charge what they're really worth.

I also joined the dots and realised that as a designer, I'm trained to do three key things...

- To be able to understand and articulate the real problems, better than those who are experiencing them.
- To visualise the situation better than it is now.
- Then, by being resourceful, relentless and unreasonable to bring that vision into existence.

So, with renewed enthusiasm and a sense of purpose, I started working with businesses to help them avoid the mistakes I'd made and achieve everything they could.

I was able to help them to see the obstacles clearly, for the first time in some cases, that were blocking their way. Giving them a greater vision of what their future could look like and uncoupling them from beliefs that held them back.

Together, we implemented strategies and systems that were so effective, they achieved real breakthroughs in days rather than years, setting those businesses on a path to unlocking significantly greater value for themselves and their clients.

On reflection, regardless of whether I was working with a newly started business or an established company making millions, the spark that unlocked their growth **always** started with their sales system and the philosophies, strategies and processes that it embodied.

One great person I worked with was an award-winning garden designer who was struggling, because he believed that each project was so complex, the sales process needed a bespoke approach, that only HE could do. Within a month he'd gone from leaving client meetings with the headache of having to labour over a proposal, to leaving the meeting with a deposit and a start date, because everything had been agreed and signed for during the meeting.

He then started to reflect on other areas of his business and to challenge those through the same lens. Resolving that first process was just the spark he needed to make him realise what was possible. The bar had been raised and he continued to raise it.

There was a local kids' football academy that had been set up by a great guy called Ben Hunter. He had been a professional footballer, playing in the MLS in America and had had this vision for an academy that could really impact children's lives through the discipline of football. However, he was struggling to effectively take payments and had no way of ever-increasing prices in the future. We worked on implementing a sales system that put them in total control.

This caused a knock-on effect of controlling other areas of their business too, which led them to a point where they could franchise. We wrote their first franchisee agreement together on the back of a napkin in Costa Coffee. Within 18 months, their revenue had grown by ten times and Kixx are now a multi-million-pound business with close to 50 franchisees.

There was a large, 8-figure revenue, waste management business. They had an established process for signing up new account customers, but it had so many needless obstacles, that it actually deterred people from signing up. When you're working with something so closely and so well established, it can be difficult to see the errors in it. With fresh eyes, we challenged and overhauled the system, developed some software and within 30 days, new account openings increased from 8 a month, to 56 a month. That business doubled their revenue over the following three years and sold (not just based on this change I hasten to add, but it certainly helped.)

During that period, I worked with over 100 businesses, across many industries, helping them to implement balanced and optimised sales systems that led to increased profits, a greater sense of control and the ability to effectively systemise other areas of their business too.

Because the sales system is so foundational, attempting to build any other system without first fully resolving it, is like trying to build a house on quicksand, during an earthquake.

Then one day, I met an accountant called Paul.

Before I move onto what happened next, I just want to add that with the money I made in the first few months of this business, I was able to go back to all the suppliers who had been out of pocket from my previous business folding, and pay them back. I believe in karma.

THE DAY I MET MAP

My Accountancy Place (now MAP) was already a great accountancy firm doing lots of things right. They were 100% cloud based, very entrepreneurial, had a specific niche of digital creative agencies and were really quite systemised.

It was owned by Paul Barnes who had first worked for a larger firm, then took on an accounting franchise and had now set up his own accounting business.

He had been on every available pricing and sales course at the time, read all the literature and set up what he believed to be a robust sales system, based on the best he'd seen within the accounting industry.

I was looking for a new accountant and had met Paul at an event. So I travelled to Manchester to check out his firm. What struck me was how sharp he was when it came to his fees. He knew how to charge, and I admired that.

Everything was calculated in an Excel spreadsheet and I could see the complex formulas working as he imputed factors about my revenue, number of staff, volume of transactions and the service I needed.

The final fee was high; three times more than I was currently paying, but what impressed me was that he'd got to the heart of what I really needed (not what I thought I wanted), his clear ability to charge a healthy fee AND his confidence to stand by it.

I admired his sales process to that point and concluded that THIS was the firm that could help to build out the finance function of my consulting business.

We got to the end of the meeting and I said "Great, where do I sign?"

He explained "It doesn't quite work like that. We have to put these agreed services and prices into an engagement letter and send it over for you to sign."

'OK.' I thought.

So, I left that meeting excited as I headed to the train station.

Now I'm from Yorkshire, where God's from, and MAP were based in Manchester, where it rains all the time.

The journey home was two hours long and I must've checked my phone ten times to see if he'd sent the proposal through, before I arrived home, but no.

When I got in, I excitedly told my wife that I'd met THE firm that was going to manage the finances of our business.

She knew how important this was for us to get right this time and to invest properly in this function.

Then came her first question "How much is it going to cost?"

I told her and she said, "Jeez, what are we getting for that?"

I said "I have no idea. But it sounded great."

(She didn't say 'jeez' by the way, it was a LOT stronger.)

Over the next two days as I waited for my proposal, my wife encouraged me to speak to other business owners I knew, to discover what they were paying their accountant, and... I talked myself out of it.

When the proposal arrived, the documentation was complicated, and I couldn't remember what everything meant or why I needed it. I was hesitant about getting on the phone again with Paul, because I now felt uncomfortable about what we'd agreed, so I ignored a few of his calls.

When he finally got hold of me two weeks later, we agreed to work together, but I wanted a few items removed from the proposal, so I felt comfortable with the fee.

When we met up again, I asked if he'd like some feedback on his sales process and he said yes.

So, I loaded both barrels.

I explained how he'd told me he was a cloud-based, digital expert, would make everything much clearer, would save me time and would help me to improve my cashflow.

My first experience however, demonstrated a *lack* of digital expertise, was not easy for me to understand, delayed the start date by over a month and showed a distinct inability to bring money into *their* business quickly.

He explained how the engagement letter software they used was the best on the market (at that time,) but it wasn't really a client facing product and could only be used by either him or Amy. They had to first copy the agreed services and prices from the spreadsheet into the system which didn't take too long, but he had been busy, and Amy only worked Tuesdays and Thursdays.

But he stood by the process saying that "Compared to most other firms, this was actually very slick."

I explained how I wasn't comparing him to other firms.

You see, I'd driven to the train station and booked my parking on my phone. As I walked to the train station, I booked my train tickets, also on my phone and when I arrived in Manchester, I ordered an Uber, on my phone too. Then when I sat in their reception, waiting for the meeting to start, I saw a book on the side which I ordered via Amazon. I was reading it the next morning with my breakfast and I still hadn't received your proposal.

You see, you're no longer being compared to other accountants or bookkeepers, you're being compared to any business I choose to compare you to, and comparatively, the experience you gave me was crap.

But I also explained how I could help.

I felt that it might be possible to take the workings of his highly evolved spreadsheet and work them into a piece of software that could present a menu of services to clients, while they were still with them in the meeting.

It could be so easy to use, that anyone on his team could work it and his clients would clearly understand how the final price and service list had been built up (without seeing the calculations.) So, if they had any questions, they could have them answered there and then, while they were still focussed on the task of signing up and had the expert next to them (not their mate down the pub.)

I also believed it would be possible to automatically use those services and prices to produce the proposal and a separate engagement letter, that would cover the required legal and regulatory aspects.

I contacted my developers and outlined the brief. I showed them the sophistication of the pricing calculations and all of the variables that would need to be considered, as well as the complexity surrounding the engagement letter.

I designed an interface that would be logical to use by anyone on the team and easy to be understood by their clients.

I then added three more parameters to the project: the entire service selection, fee agreement and sign-off process must be completable in under 5 minutes; by their most junior member of staff; having had no more than 10 minutes of training.

Without setting these parameters, I knew it would just be another thing that gets implemented and never used.

We called it the **'5 Minute Proposal Tool'** (catchy) and I really never thought any more of it. It was just another sales system I'd implemented into another business. It had more complexity around the pricing and compliance aspects, but it really just encapsulated everything I'd been working on for the past decade in other businesses.

Based on the impact that software had, on what was already a well running firm, we were able to implement the remaining 6 systems I'd identified as being critical, in any highly effective business.

That work led to Paul making me a Director of MAP and giving me a 10% shareholding.

A friend of mine at the time had been working to help systemise another very entrepreneurial accounting business called Northern Accountants. They'd heard about the proposal software we'd developed at MAP and wanted it too.

And that was the spark that made me think this had the potential to become a commercial product, for the accounting industry.

There was nothing available that was truly client facing, had that level of pricing sophistication and could genuinely be completed in minutes.

This product and accompanying philosophies were unique in that it had been pressure tested, forged and honed in profit-driven businesses for years, outside of the accounting industry. These merged with the proven, industry specific pricing methodologies that Paul had refined and **GoProposal** was born.

As the product began to gather momentum, I scaled back the other work I was doing, to focus all of my learnings and experience into this one industry; helping accountants and bookkeepers to stand shoulder to shoulder with their clients and to create mutually valuable relationships.

We began working with accounting businesses around the world, helping them to fundamentally grow more profitably.

We typically get accountants doubling, tripling and quadrupling their fees and there are two reasons that excites me:

ONE - I know that **you're** getting paid for all the hard work that you do. If you don't charge enough, you can't deliver the level of service that your clients are happy to pay for.

TWO - I know that your **clients** are receiving the services they need from you, in order to grow more predictably and avoid the experience that I went through when my business failed.

As the Director of MAP, I also get to share everything that is already working in a systemised, profitable, efficient and growing firm of accountants. Where the owner is working ON the business and not IN it. Half of our growth comes from existing clients and half comes from new clients.

I have now taught these philosophies and strategies to literally thousands of firms around the world as the keynote speaker at events, via videos, through our academy, our community and our software. I have had one-to-one conversations and training sessions in person and via Zoom with hundreds and hundreds of firms and individuals.

I have spoken to them about their challenges and had the privilege to witness first-hand, the positive impact we've been able to have.

Everything I'm sharing with you here works, now, today, in a post-cloud, post-Covid, highly competitive world.

My mission is to empower the world's accounting businesses to build the most valuable relationships with their clients.

That's me. That's my why.

"The reasonable man adapts himself to the world; the unreasonable one persists to adapt the world to himself. Therefore, all progress depends on the unreasonable man."

- George Bernard Shaw

THE 7 SYSTEMS

Before we dive into the sales system specifically, I've already alluded to the fact that there are 6 others, so I want to first outline what ALL of the 7 systems are of a highly effective firm.

You see, everyone talks about 'systemising' your business, but then fail to tell you *which* systems you need. And the challenge of implementing systems is how to build them so they STICK.

We've all experienced the frustration of introducing a new process to your business, only to see it fade away after a short while.

I always liken it to rebuilding the same part of a wall over and over again. Building systems in a business can very much feel like building the first few rows of a wall, then they get knocked down and you have to rebuild them again with the next idea and the next. But it just never seems to gain height. It's tiring.

This happens when we don't get everyone's buy-in, because they don't know why we're doing it in the first place or how they will benefit when it's in place.

It's just another crazy idea from you, they think. Let's go along with it for a while and you'll soon drop it like everything else.

For systems to work effectively, they need to include…

☐   **A why.** Why are we doing this in the first place. How do the clients, the team and the business benefit?

☐ **A checklist.** This is simply a list of tasks that ensures all the correct things happen every time, to the correct standards. This could be an automated series of events.

☐ **A check for the checklist.** Anything you expect, you have to inspect, so there needs to be a checking process in place to ensure the standards are met.

☐ **An improvement strategy.** Nothing ever stays the same and left unchecked, it will be getting worse. So, you have to actively improve your processes with an appropriate rhythm, such as every quarter. Without this, the rows of bricks in the system get knocked down or fall down.

If you want consistently high results, your systems need these elements.

Now let me outline the 7 systems we have in place in our firm and which have helped us to provide greater value, wow our clients and build a scalable business.

1. THE ATTRACTION SYSTEM

This is where you identify your dream prospects and attract them in their highest quantity and quality into your firm. If you don't know who you want, you can't really complain when you don't get them.

2. THE NURTURE SYSTEM

This is where you connect with those prospects and nurture them over time to the point where they make it clear that they want your services. This is rarely in place and a huge sinkhole of lost opportunities. Our nurture processes are 12 months long for new prospects.

3. THE SALES SYSTEM

This is where you turn a prospect into a client and upgrade existing clients into buying more from you. It's where you define the relationship you intend to have with a prospect, wean out the time wasters, propose to them and convert them into your dream client. Without a sale, no value can be exchanged and so this is fundamental to the growth of your business. It's the one most people avoid, but the one that has the potential to have the greatest impact and where we should always start. This is the one we're going to be locking down.

4. THE ONBOARDING SYSTEM

This is where you wow your new clients by making it super smooth to onboard them with minimal pain for them and you. This is their first interaction with your practice and so it's important that you nail it. It's also where you onboard existing clients into new services. We've got this process totally locked down and delivering high levels of wow already.

5. THE DELIVERY SYSTEM

This is how you ultimately deliver your service to your clients. It's where you maximise the lifetime value you provide to them by procedurising, planning and doing the work. All of the low-level activities are put on autopilot and your team are freed up to work on their highest value activities, with high levels of accuracy and fast turnaround times. Get this right and you will form deep and meaningful partnerships with your clients, where you're an intrinsic part of their success.

6. THE FINANCE SYSTEM

This is where you continually maximise your income by ensuring that you're pricing profitably and have THE most robust payment system that automates the flow of cash from your clients to you. Without this in place, you will be leaking profits, leaving money on the table and the more clients you get, the worse it will be. This system is the one you must be an expert in because it's ultimately where you're helping your clients to achieve financial maturity too. But you don't have the right to help your clients to achieve this, until you've mastered it yourself first.

7. THE STAFFING SYSTEM

This is where you attract, recruit and grow the best people that perfectly fit your culture and your aspirations. You can't grow your business; all you can do is grow your people and *they* will grow your business. This only works if you have robust systems in the first place with no cracks and a clearly defined set of useful core values.

WHY DO WE SYSTEMISE?

There are several reasons why you'd want to systemise your accountancy firm, but most people miss the ultimate reason why we do it.

So let me outline some of the reasons why you need to systemise your business and then I'll reveal what I believe to be the BIG one. This is the one that rarely, if ever, gets talked about but the one that has the greatest impact on your clients for one specific reason.

1. CONTROL THE CHAOS

As any business grows, it naturally becomes more and more chaotic. You take on more people, learn new methods of doing things, encounter new challenges, get more clients and offer more services and with every new thing we add into our business, the chaos compounds. Systemising your business controls that chaos and returns calm to our lives.

2. FRANCHISE YOUR PRACTICE

Once your business is fully systemized, you have effectively installed the 'franchisable model' into your firm, so it *could* be franchised out. This could be on a large scale or it could just be something you do with a few practices in nearby towns. But the main driver for achieving this is not because you have to franchise, but to give you choices. A business that can be franchised must be fully systemised, be replicable, produce predictable, repeatable results, be fully documented, have protected IP and have removed you from the day-to-day running of it. By getting to this point, you just have more choices and options in your life.

3. SCALE YOUR PRACTICE

Without true systems being installed in your business, scaling would be a nightmare. Each customer you attempt to bring in would widen the cracks, increase the chaos, add to the overwhelm and exaggerate the problems. Some accountants think that if they just push through it will all come good. It won't.

4. REMOVE THE OVERWHELM

Most firms have people running their practice and so they naturally become overwhelmed. This is because people should not be running your practice. Systems should be running your practice and people should be running the systems. Do it the other way around and overwhelm will increase.

5. REDUCE YOUR VULNERABILITY

Without proper systems, you're vulnerable because if someone leaves, you're in deep water. But if you have systems running your business and that person was running the system, it makes you far less vulnerable. Of course, there will be other problems you'll need to deal with, but your vulnerability will be less. Proper systems also reduce the risk of someone making a mistake either accidentally or intentionally. There should be sufficient checks in place that prevent your clients, the jobs and key tasks from falling through the cracks.

6. MAXIMISE THE VALUE

Without a fully systemised, crack-free business, there's no way you can be maximising the lifetime value of your clients. Do all of your clients know everything you do? Have you carried out an audit on what services they will need over the next three years? Are there mechanisms in place, which are moving those clients towards those additional services that they need? If not, the great news is that most of this can be automated IF the systems are right.

7. SELL YOUR PRACTICE

A fully systemised business with the correct technology, automation (where appropriate), instructional manuals and training programs make your business far more saleable AND worth a lot more. Systemisation and scalability can increase the value of your firm by several times more than that of a normal practice.

8. ALLOW YOU TO STEP BACK

Maybe you don't want to do any of those things, but you just want to step back and let the business run itself, with little input from you. Systemising allows that to happen. I speak to 50 and 60 year old firm owners who love what they do, but think they have to retire soon. Why? You're going to live far longer than you think, so why not keep going? Think what you could do with your business over the next 30 years. You're just getting warmed up. Get it running without you first, then step back and just get involved in strategy or marketing or whatever you enjoy most. Rather than build to a day where you retire, take continual retirements until you're 90. Working one day a week or one week a month. Don't stop now. Keep going.

THE BIG ONE

So here's the biggy. We systemise our business for one main reason and it's one that is rarely considered by the majority of businesses, let alone accountancy firms.

You should systemise in order to **provide incredible experiences to your clients.**

That's it.

That's why we do it.

Your clients will remember how you made them feel, long after they've forgotten what you've done for them, and we change the way they feel through the experiences we provide. But we cannot even begin to consider this ultimate level until we have everything else in place, the service we're providing is outstanding and the value we provide has been maximised.

Incredible experiences are where the game is won.

THE SALES SYSTEM

The sales system is the key to unlocking the success of all other systems, but it's also the one that's disliked and so tends to be avoided.

It's disliked because a lot of us have some negative association with selling, because of experiences we've had in the past. And selling, especially to highly skilled, highly talented accountants and bookkeepers, seems beneath them.

What I want to do throughout the course of this book is to reverse that thinking and share with you a totally different approach to selling, helping you to discover that it is in fact one of THE greatest skills you can have in your firm and life.

To sell is truly to serve. It's about understanding your client's weaknesses and discovering how you can strengthen them. It is what allows you to deliver the maximum value you possibly can to your clients.

Without it being firmly in place and fully understood by everyone in your organisation, I guarantee that you will have existing clients who aren't receiving the most value they possibly could from you, and you will have allowed prospects to have never become clients in the first place.

To sell is your ethical obligation and I will be showing you how, with the correct system, most of the legwork can be done for you so it won't feel like selling at all. Done right, people will buy better levels of service from you, for higher fees and with greater frequency.

But above all of that, the sales system is **pivotal** in determining the success of the relationship moving forwards. Now that's not to take anything away from the systems before or after this one, as all of them are important if your practice is to be a success.

But this one system transitions a prospect into a client; it takes someone who is already a good fit for you and turns them into a fee-paying client.

It sets the tone for everything to follow and determines the parameters for a successful (or doomed) relationship.

But before I can properly map it out for you, I need you to reflect on what you have in place now and the challenges that lay around that. I also want to point out the difference between prospects and clients, proposals and engagement letters.

PROSPECTS OR EXISTING CLIENTS

Selling can either be to prospects, with the view of turning them into clients or it can be to sell additional services to existing clients.

Out of those two types of sales, selling to existing clients is far easier. If I had to help you to make more money today, I would concentrate on your existing clients, because that's where the greatest potential and immediate results lie.

Half of the sales in our accounting business come from existing clients and the other half from new clients.

The sales process I will be outlining in this book will be to new prospects. That's because it's the harder and more thorough of the two processes. It requires more steps to establish trust, indoctrinate them into our way of thinking and generate a sense of certainty; existing clients should already have this.

But a simplified process can be equally applied to existing clients.

You can still arrange a discovery call with an existing client to discuss whether an additional service is a good fit for them, for example.

You can still arrange an annual GLOSS review with an existing client to ensure their goals, location and obstacles are still the same.

From now on, when you think of **sales**, just think of *new prospects* **and** *existing clients* equally.

PROPOSAL VS ENGAGEMENT LETTER

Before I outline the typical process, I just want to clear up the difference between proposals and engagement letters for the purpose of this discussion.

A proposal is an offer for consideration. Put simply, it says, this is what we're promising we're going to do, in exchange for this fee.

This proposal could be verbal, in an email, a video, as a separate document or contained *within* the engagement letter.

The engagement letter outlines the key responsibilities of each party, ensures you are meeting your regulatory and compliance obligations and protects you and the client from risk.

Both documents have clearly separate functions and should always be split out.

The proposal is where you communicate the value exchange. Its primary function is to close the sale.

The engagement letter protects you and the client legally (although it has the potential to be so much more useful if done properly.)

If you add the proposal within the engagement letter, it will be overlooked, and the client will struggle to understand the value you're promising.

For the best possible client experience and the most efficient process, both documents must be separate, produced up front and sent together.

Some people believe in sending a proposal first, and if accepted, to send the engagement letter second. This, to my mind, puts needless obstacles in the way and prevents the client from having all the information they need to make a decision.

Now you may say that an engagement letter can't be issued until legal checks are carried out on this client, such as Anti-Money Laundering or Professional Clearance.

However, it is possible to engage a client without having these done on the assumption that they will pass, and then to disengage the client if they don't.

Or you can send the engagement letter and have it signed, but state they are not formally engaged until all clearances have been made, at which time, you then send the finalised letter and engage the client.

Either way, the point I'm making is this process can be radically streamlined and can still be done legally and compliantly.

I invite you to challenge your current process.

'We do it this way because we've always done it this way,' is not a valid reason… it's an excuse.

TYPICAL SALES PROCESSES

An effective system is a complete set of processes with no cracks between them. The goal of building any system is to remove the cracks. That's it, that's enough, we don't have to get fancy.

I use the word 'processes' here, because rarely do *any* businesses have a complete sales 'system' in place, let alone accounting businesses.

So, let me outline how those typical sales processes work, so you can see the fundamental flaws and the opportunities for massive improvement.

1. INTEREST IS REGISTERED

So typically, somebody registers their interest in your service and raises their hand to say that they want to talk to you about your services.

This hand raising may come in the form of an email or a phone call but normally sounds something like this:

"Hi, I have a business and I'm currently looking for a new accountant. I've checked out your website and wondered what you charge? Could we have a chat to discuss? Cheers, James"

You may feel pressured to give an indicative price at this point. That's a mistake and when they ask "what do you charge" that's not what they're really asking.

2. A MEETING IS ARRANGED

You then may call them or reply to the email and you may even ask them a few probing questions, but essentially you arrange a meeting to discuss their requirements, regardless of whether they're going to be a good fit or not.

Typically, the response back to the client is delayed, especially if they've contacted you on a Saturday morning for example, and the meeting is always arranged without any qualification.

You're saying (eventually), here, have an hour of our time.

3. THE MEETING OCCURS

Then in around a week's time, you have an hour-long meeting where you learn more about their business and perhaps even deliver a presentation about yours.

You may have some standard questions, which you ask...or you may not.

You may also have some sort of pricing tool which can give them a good indication of costs there and then...or you may not.

You then promise to send them a proposal outlining costs, which you then email to them over the next few days.

This meeting rarely has a fixed agenda and nearly always overruns.

4. A PROPOSAL IS SENT

You then spend time producing the proposal and/or a letter of engagement which outlines the costs and scope of the work you plan to do for them.

On a more basic level, this could just be an email outlining the above.

This whole process normally takes longer than you promised, and the documents are perhaps not as thorough as you'd like them to be.

You may have to get the documentation cross checked to make sure the pricing is correct, which takes more time.

The proposal is also probably not a compelling sales tool that wows the client, but hey ho, it's done.

You send it through, late, with your fingers crossed having little idea whether it will land within the client's expectations.

5. YOU FOLLOW UP

At an undetermined time in the future, you or a member of your team then calls to see if they want to go ahead.

This normally takes several attempts and if it's any more than five, you will give up, assuming they're not interested, or you just don't want to come across as pushy.

If you do get hold of them, they may want to amend the services, clarify what certain services are, or ask for a discount. At that point, they may sign up or not.

If they don't, well not to worry, we won't chase them because we don't want to be seen as pestering them.

6. YOU SIGN THEM UP

You may have a system that permits the client to sign digitally.

If not, then the client will need to check their printer has ink cartridges, order some if not, print out the documentation, sign it, find an envelope (they don't have an envelope), go to the post office (eventually) and return it to you.

But let's assume they *can* sign the proposal digitally.

This normally then requires some manual step of taking the costs from the proposal and sending it through to prospect to be signed electronically...which they hopefully do.

If they don't sign, you'll probably give them a nudge at some point... probably.

They finally sign the proposal and whoever gets notified in the firm, will then inform the people who will start the ball rolling with onboarding... maybe.

And that's it.

That's the normal process and it seems reasonable enough right?

Wrong.

And it's so wrong that I would anticipate that if your process sounds similar to this, then you are creating yourself a whole world of pain further down the line.

If it's this hard to get the initial proposal created, signed and accepted, it's no wonder that fee reviews get postponed. It's more painful to go through this process than just to run those extra payrolls for free, right?

WHAT'S WRONG WITH THIS PROCESS

Let me break this down, outline the major problems with this process and share a different approach.

1. THE INITIAL INTEREST

So, somebody registers his or her interest in your service. This is the one chance you have to take control of the situation. It's the opportunity you have to stamp your authority on the relationship and reassure them that they have just found **the** expert that can provide what they're looking for. You have one chance to nail this.

The mistake made here is the time lag between raising interest and it being acknowledged. Maybe it's a Saturday morning or Sunday evening when they choose to reach out. Do they expect an immediate response? Absolutely.

2. ARRANGING THE MEETING

They want a meeting with you, but the problem with that is... you don't know whether you want a meeting with them.

What's the point of tying up your precious time if you don't know if they're a precise fit for your firm and whether or not you can provide them with the value they need?

So, you need a step in here that determines this fit, removes the time wasters but also doesn't scare off your dream customers. The balancing act in getting this right is pivotal in making the rest of this system work.

But let's say they get past that phase and everything seems rosy. What typically happens between *arranging the meeting* and *having the meeting* is... nothing.

Sure, you might be forward thinking enough to send out a reminder email. Hell, you may even by firing out SMS text reminders, but typically that's it.

This is a massively wasted opportunity to start the selling of your services.

Why waste the time between *arranging* the meeting and *having* the meeting? This is a real opportunity to move the relationship forward.

Wouldn't it be a different situation if this prospect was turning up to buy from you rather than to be sold to.

And what if that all occurred automatically, without you having to lift a finger?

So, assuming you don't have that, this time is wasted; time you, and they, don't have.

3. THE MEETING

This is your first real date, where first impressions are everything.

Normally, a senior member of the team conducts the sales meeting. Their goal is to take them from 0 to 100 in the space of an hour (0 is where they don't really know how you can help them and 100 is where they're signed up, certain that you can.)

So, we've tied up one of our most valuable assets to complete a near impossible task...but it gets better.

This senior accountant is then going to spend the next 40 minutes trying to figure out what's going on in their business and what challenges they're facing. This is very difficult to do if you don't have a consultative sales framework and you will likely end up offering this client what they *want*, rather than what they really *need*.

You will attempt to sell a collection of services, perhaps based on what you've offered the last ten prospects you spoke to and do your best to sell the benefits of each one.

Now if you're worth your salt, you should be charging a fair whack for what you do, certainly more than the competitors. So you have this uphill struggle of pitching something more expensive than everyone else, to someone you know little about.

If the meeting doesn't have an agenda which you control, the client will take control instead. I guarantee this will lead to the meeting overrunning, and what this communicates to the client is that **your time has no value.**

But let's say there is an agenda, and you've arrived at the point where you're discussing exactly what they need.

At this point, I really hope that you have a method of presenting the precise scope and associated fees to your clients, so you can have that in-depth pricing discussion with them. Even if it's in an excel spreadsheet. The reality is that most firms don't and it's shaky at best.

If it's shaky in any way, this is where the client may push you for a discount or where you may end up giving away additional services for free, which is a fatal mistake (you'll see why.)

If you're unable to agree to the services, precise service levels, and fees while they're still with you, and… if you can't produce a proposal and a letter of engagement there and then, you can't get anything agreed with the client, which was the point of the meeting.

You have their full and undivided attention in that meeting. When they walk out the door, they're checking emails, calling the office, picking the kids up from school; they're gone.

The purpose of this meeting was to get an agreement on what you're going to do for them, answer any questions that need answering and ideally sign them up, or at least take them as far as you comfortably can.

But instead, you let them go with nothing agreed and without confirming when you're going to call them next. You are now relying on the hope; hope that what you're proposing is right and hope that you will call at the precise moment when they'll be ready to make a decision.

Good luck with that.

4. THE PROPOSAL

Now comes the fun part.

That proposal that you said you'd have sent by the end of the week has taken a little longer than you anticipated to produce. It's not quite as good as you would have liked it to have been because you haven't got round to 'tidying it up' yet.

It still contains elements which have led to problems with other clients in the past, so will be likely to cause problems with this one too, but you hope it won't. Maybe it had to be approved by someone else. Were they available to approve it? Did that slow things down further?

It gets sent out with a semi-plausible excuse as to why it's late. This annoys the hell out the prospect and is the first promise broken. It's like turning up to your second date, two days late.

The ability to command high fees is now on shakier ground than before, but the process continues.

This proposal outlines the costs and… well that's it, it outlines the costs and this proposal looks like every other proposal that every other accountant has ever sent, because a proposal is just a proposal, right? Wrong.

This proposal is your salesperson in the room after you've walked out. This proposal now has a tough job to do, and if it's not designed to nail the deal, then you're going to be losing potential dream customers. If you got this right, as well as convincing them to sign up for your services, it could also be encouraging them to sign up for more services.

They don't just need you to upsell them... they could upsell themselves, if the document and your process is designed to do that.

5. THE FOLLOW UP

The follow up is where most firms allow money to literally trickle through their fingers. This might be following up with a new prospect or following up with an existing client for an additional service.

Firstly, you need to know exactly WHEN to follow up. You must not leave this to chance.

You needed to have known who else they needed to consult with in order to make a decision, how long it would take them to make that decision and when was the best time to call them back.

If you were unable to contact them, you concluded this meant something, such as they're not interested. It means nothing other than you weren't able to contact them. Any other assumption is likely to be fear based and needs to be challenged.

But let's say they're either not interested now, or you genuinely couldn't get hold of them, you still need a long-term follow up process in place, because what if they're just not ready to sign up this year? What if they want to stay where they are for 12 more months because their accountant's their friend and they don't want to upset them.

So, it's fair to say that the follow up doesn't occur and if it does, it's broken. Is that fair?

6. THE SIGN UP

So this process for many accountants (if you have it online) appears fairly robust and in isolation, it probably is.

But it falls down in its ability to smoothly transition someone from *wanting* to sign up to *actually* signing up, because there is normally a manual process in creating the engagement letter.

Engagement letters by their nature are very complex documents with a huge responsibility to protect both parties from risk. They communicate key responsibilities and ensure the highest standards of professional compliance are being met. They should contain specific service schedules related to the agreed services, outline key dates related to those services and perfectly reflect the precise circumstances of your firm. And certainly, in the UK, an appropriate liability cap needs to be agreed with the client to limit your liability, otherwise you can be exposed to unlimited liability.

All of these things take time to get right and normally, only a few people within your firm will have that level of knowledge to produce this document to the correct level of accuracy.

This may delay the process by a significant amount of time, or else rushed, leaving you exposed to unnecessary risk.

Where it can fail completely is if they don't sign. What then? What mechanisms do you have in place to ensure that it does get signed?

If it does get signed, the system then typically breaks again and reveals another crack as it transitions into your onboarding processes (presuming you have them.)

We once signed a HUGE client into our firm that would have been by far our largest client at that point. Everything in the sign-up process had gone smoothly, but then we completely messed up the onboarding meeting and the start of that process. Despite the fact that the client had signed up, they walked away. The great experience **must** continue.

Now maybe all of this doesn't seem all that bad, but this isn't even the worst part.

IT GETS WORSE....

There are additional problems that are created in this process, that may not have been evident at first glance.

Firstly, the whole process is drawn out and prevents the right person from signing up there and then. You can go out and buy a car today, so why not accountancy services?

Secondly, it ties up some of the most knowledgeable and senior members of your team, whose time could be better spent elsewhere, making you money.

Thirdly, there is a disconnect between the promises sold during that sales meeting by the Senior Team Member and the service that then ensues, which is typically delivered by someone else. This leads to a sense of underwhelm for the client and overwhelm for your team.

You are also restricted with the number of sales meetings that can take place, because you only have one or two people who can deliver an effective presentation and pitch.

And don't forget, the majority of the sales meetings you should be having are with existing clients who desperately need more from you.

The whole experience for the prospect or client, doesn't leave them feeling wowed. This makes it more challenging to sell them what they *really* need for the fees they need to pay.

But all of this... all of these problems pale into the background when you understand the enormity of the real problem that it compounds.

A problem which is undermining your entire firm, causing all of your team to feel overwhelmed, minimising the value you can provide to your clients, increasing your churn rate, reducing your profits, restricting your referrals and basically causing 80% of the headaches throughout your firm.

THE REAL PROBLEM

The real problem you've just created is in allowing the prospect to take control of the process and to behave how they want. You have relinquished all authority throughout the process and handed the power to them.

They are now in control of your business.

You have communicated that your time has no value, and if you give a discount or **anything** away for free, then your services have no value either.

Effectively, you've said.... Here are the keys, you're in charge, our time has no value, our services have no value.

And what's your biggest frustration with your clients? That they underpay you, undervalue you, you're overworked, they never do as you ask them, which leads to total chaos and you're overwhelmed.

The knock-on effect is that if you're lucky enough to sign them as a client (and the above method is based entirely on luck) they will continue to behave as they want to and to take control over the relationship.

It's like if I asked my children what they want to eat, what they want to do and when they want to go to bed.

The answer would be garbage, play Fortnite and never.

But as a loving parent, I have to be kind to them by being in charge of the relationship and setting boundaries.

Naughty children aren't born, they're created. Bad clients don't turn up, they're created.

They're created when we confuse being kind with being nice.

I'm being kind to my children when I send them to bed on time, even if *they don't think* I'm being nice, because they want to watch DanTDM on YouTube for the millionth time that day.

If your client is in total control of the relationship, it's because of how **you** have allowed the relationship to be formed.

So, when they don't reconcile their accounts on time, or they fail to raise those invoices and they rock up to your office with a carrier bag, full of receipts and tell you to sort it out… you can't really complain.

When your team's precious time is taken up chasing these clients, increasing turnaround times and preventing you from delivering higher value services, you can't really tell your client off.

When your client then turns round and says the value you're providing me is not what you promised, you're terrible, I'm off… you can't really blame them.

But let me get you off the hook too, because you're not to blame either.

I'm sure you're great at the work you do.

I'm sure your intentions are good and that your genuine goal is to provide great value to your clients.

It's just that the world has changed and your competition is no longer other accountants.

As I explained earlier, your competition is anyone I choose to compare you to.

If I've been onto Amazon's website on a Saturday night and ordered a book and it arrives the following day... on a Sunday morning, and then I come and meet you and it takes you a week to send me a proposal... rightly or wrongly, fairly or unfairly, I'm comparing you to Amazon.

You now need to be thinking about being **world-class**, not just the best firm in your town, because your clients have more power and higher expectations than ever before. Geographical boundaries have fallen away.

You need to be able to maximise the lifetime value you bring to them and deliver it through world-class experiences... or you're going to lose to someone else who does.

The massive problem you created, started when you first allowed the prospect to take control of the process.

The good news for you, is that this process can be corrected and has already been proven.

It places you as *the authority* in the relationship, enables you to confidently present the client with what they need, not just what they want, allows you to command much higher fees, uses no weird, outdated, sales psychology, will be adopted by your entire team, you will be loved by your clients and it will be very efficient to run.

I have the blueprint that lays it all out and the tools that will accelerate the process. But... just having the blueprint, the strategy, the map, won't solve your problems.

You see, the blueprint is only 20% of your problem, 80% is psychological; **your** psychology, the psychology of your partners and that of your team.

Unless everyone's mindset is perfectly aligned with the strategy, nothing moves forward, and you'll blame the strategy. And when it comes to selling, the deepest parts of your psyche are involved; parts that have been evolving for millions of years and which are designed to prevent you from doing the very things you must do.

It would be easy for me to just give you the map and wish you well on your way, but that wouldn't be being fair to you. I actually want you to use it; I want to make a real difference.

I want you to be able to take the action you need and arrive at the gold you're looking for.

I want to impact your business and ultimately your life and for that, you'll need the mindset too.

PART II
THE MINDSET

FIRST THINGS FIRST

I promise I am going to give you the step-by-step blueprint to the sales system I've helped many firms around the world to successfully implement… no strings.

I'm talking every stage mapped out, exactly what to say at each stage, the technology to use, the objections you'll hit and how to overcome them.

I'll also give you the fast-track version of turning this on.

But before I give you it, you need to understand why the blueprint alone won't work.

You see, the blueprint is a map to the gold.

But for this map to work, it must be aligned with your mindset.

If they're not aligned, you'll never move forward, and it will actually cause you more frustration. This is because you will have glimpsed what's possible but not understand why it's eluding you.

The map in fact, is the easy part.

I could show you right now how to increase your fees by 20% without doing any more work and losing very few clients, if any.

I can give you examples of where firms have gone to their top paying clients and increased their fees by up to 10 times by providing higher levels of service, even if they've rejected fee increases in the past.

I can show you how to become THE authority in your client relationships so they value you more and do what you want them to do, when you want it doing, in the way you want it done.

But… before we can consider any of that, we must first unravel years of conflicting thinking, limiting beliefs, social conditioning, misinformation and even the oldest parts of your hardwiring.

We need to challenge your mindset at its core.

We need to really get under the skin of what selling really means and reinterpret your relationship with money.

We need to look at the fear of rejection and why that drives you to make some of the decisions you make.

We need to go deep.

And as we go on this journey, you need to be open and prepared to challenge your thinking. Because we are going to unravel some of your greatest internal conflicts when it comes to selling and valuing yourself. Once they're unravelled, it will be easy to align them with the blueprint you're going to be given at the end.

Strap in. It's going to get bumpy.

WHY YOU *REALLY* THINK SELLING IS BAD

Let's go straight to the core of the problem... most accountants, bookkeepers and CPAs think it's wrong to sell. They think that somehow, to sell to their clients, the services they need, is either *unethical* or *beneath* a trained professional.

It's as though the qualification you received made you exempt from selling; something that humans have been doing since the beginning of time.

It wasn't that long ago that accounting firms weren't even allowed to market themselves. And that legacy has persisted so that now, many firms still see selling as somehow against the rules and unprofessional.

But selling isn't just about money.

We're selling all of the time.

You sell *the idea* of why your clients need to file their tax return on time.

You sell them *the benefits* of using cloud software over desktop software.

You sell them *the accuracy* of data so they can make more informed, timely decisions.

So, if you would passionately and legitimately stand up for why it's right to 'sell' in all of these cases, why is it wrong to sell them the services they need too?

Is it because the accounting industry's perception of selling and how to do it professionally and ethically, is out of date?

Is it because it's wrongly assumed that if you're selling, you're trying to get money from people who don't want to give it or don't have it?

Has it in fact got nothing to do with this and **everything to do with how selling would make you feel if you were to get it wrong?**

Or is it to do with the fact that you were led to believe that when you got your qualifications, people would just drop at your feet and say yes to everything you had to offer, just because of your expertise?

Or is it a bit of all of these?

Let's dig deeper.

THEIR PROBLEM IS NOT THEIR *REAL* PROBLEM

Your clients face one very *real* problem and it's never the one they tell you about.

So, what most firms do is listen to the problem the client presents them with, and then attempt to sell them services to solve that problem.

The firm may be smarter than that and may use a consultative sales process such as our GLOSS Method® (more on that later) to dig deeper with their clients and uncover even bigger problems.

But rarely do they ever get to what the *real* problem is.

I propose that the *real problem* is that **they can't decide what to do** about their problem.

Most people just can't decide. And if they're really struggling financially and have pain associated with the finance function of their business or with their previous accountant, this is made even worse. All of these factors corrode the confidence they have in their decision-making ability.

And if you were to offer your client three choices about which set of services they'd prefer, you plunge them into a world of procrastination.

Giving them too many choices fills them with fear and doubt about making the wrong decision.

Your clients can live with financial pain, but they can't live with the uncertainty that comes with taking risk. And starting to work with you or taking on that additional service represents risk.

You see, we're never trained in how to make good decisions and how to be comfortable with taking risk (which is what a client is doing when choosing to work with you or to buy more from you.)

The trap you can fall into is believing that because you are qualified and you know what you're doing, then you don't have to sell. But your clients are not as interested in your qualifications as you are, they are interested in themselves.

In fact, the reality is that many of them don't know what you do. They've either believed in the adverts from the accounting software companies and think it's all just a click of a button now, right? Or they think that accounting is just so complicated (and all about confusing maths and unfathomable reports and spreadsheets,) that they just don't want to consider what you do. Either way, one thing's for sure… your clients and prospects aren't really sure what you do.

So now we're getting close to the real problem.

If they're unsure, it means they're uncertain. If they're uncertain, they're unlikely to decide until they're made to feel more certain. And that's all we're really trying to do when we sell, which is to help them to feel more certain about their decision to work with you or to buy more from you. But something else is required to help more clients to make that decision in the first place.

The thing they need is *certainty in the outcome* and this is only achieved when they're sold to, in a way that is ethical and professional and makes them feel good about what you're going to do for them.

Before you can help your clients to improve the finance function of their business or to file their personal tax return, you must first help them to make a decision.

To sell is to help people to make better decisions faster. It's **not** about taking money from people. This is an important distinction you must make. When you do that, you will feel more confident in selling.

Change your view that 'selling is about how to take money from your clients.' Instead, replace it with the view that 'selling is about helping them to feel confident in spending the money they need to invest in building a more financially sound business.'

Start to reinterpret what you think of as 'selling', to be solving your client's real problem, which is their inability to decide. When you do, you will serve a lot more people to a much higher level.

Selling is your ethical obligation. You must get comfortable with this.

If you avoid selling somebody something that they really need, whose interests are you really putting first?

WHY YOU DON'T LIKE ASKING FOR MONEY

Have you ever done this?

You complete a piece of work for a client. Maybe it's something relatively small that didn't take you that long.

But after completing the work, for some reason, you don't feel comfortable asking for money, so you say that on this occasion, there's no charge.

You kindly tell them that if this work needs to be done again, then *you might have to charge them*, but on this occasion, you're going to discount the price of your service to zero.

You justify it to yourself in the name of *wanting to help them*. But is that the truth or is there something else going on?

Many people I've spoken to over the years in this space, tell me that they don't like to sell and that they don't feel comfortable asking for money.

Some are even proud of the fact that they go above and beyond and provide all of these extras for free. They *just want to do good…* right?

But is that truly accurate?

I know they're a good person. I know that deep down they want to help and serve. I'm not doubting that. But could it be that what they're really saying is that they don't know *how* to ask for payment without feeling like they're being judged, or risking being rejected?

There's a big difference and it's a very important awareness to have.

When we start to get under the skin of this, we start to see the real reason people don't like selling. It's because it puts you in an awkward position where you could be judged as being 'salesy' or 'greedy' or 'unfair'. All of these make you feel bad about yourself and if you've ever experienced that feeling, even just once, you'll do everything you can to avoid it again.

You make the mistake of thinking that if you take money from them, they're not going to be able to feed their kids or they're going to be homeless. As if getting their bookkeeping completed accurately means that they will have to go without, and you'd be the one responsible for them starving or rendering them homeless. But this is completely made up, only going on in your head and over catastrophised in your mind.

Your mind will do everything it can to protect you. It has been evolving for millions of years and has learned every trick in the book to manipulate you into avoiding actions that could possibly involve pain. So, if it knows you've felt bad about asking for money in the past, it will fabricate stories in your mind as to why you should avoid this again, even if they're untrue.

Does this resonate?

So, the root fear you have about selling, really comes down to your fear of rejection and fear of being judged.

Your qualifications, training and experience have raised you up, which you think would help. But it only makes things worse, because now you're in a much higher position in your mind, to fall from. Rejection from this height will really hurt!!!

It's not that you don't want to charge for your services, it's that you don't want to discover that they don't want to pay for them.

If your fees are rejected, YOU feel rejected, which can make you feel inferior. This is hardwired into your brain and designed to keep you part of the tribe.

Avoid rejection, stay a part of the tribe and you'll live.

Be rejected and you'll be put outside of the tribe and have to fend for yourself, meaning that you'll likely die.

That stuff is hard coded and was put into your brain to prevent you from being eaten by sabre tooth tigers. But the world has evolved far faster than our brains have, and so that fear mechanism is no longer needed, but still there.

And you can't get rid of that feeling of rejection.... EVER! So, your mind concludes that you should avoid any scenario where that could be a possibility, altogether.

One way to avoid that feeling is to accept the excuse they give you as to why they can't pay for your services, whatever it is. That's your **get out of pain card**, so you're quick to take it and deep down, you are relieved.

If you present a set of services to your clients that you know they really need, and they say they can't afford them or say they don't have time right now, it's easy to say it's *their issue* and has *nothing to do with you.* And in doing so, you take yourself out of the firing line of possible rejection. *Phew.... the reason they said no was entirely to do with them, not me.*

But the real reason you're quick to accept their excuse is because you don't want to confront the fact that their real concern *might* be you.

Instead of considering that there might be some other reason for their objection, and ethically challenging it, it's easier to accept that price is their real issue and to buy into the story that they have no money (even though they have a new BMW on the drive, a 70" plasma TV on the wall, all their kids have iPhones and they've just booked an extravagant family holiday.)

IS MONEY EVER THE ISSUE?

Money is rarely the issue.

The number one reason your clients won't buy from you is because they don't want to make another bad decision, and unless you can give them certainty in the outcome, that's what they fear will happen; spending money and not getting the outcome they want.

They won't say that, because they don't know that's why themselves. But they will say it's too expensive or it's more than they wanted to spend or worse.... they won't say anything at all.

But they're not struggling to buy the latest iPhone or to spend thousands on Amazon for stuff they don't really need.

The fact of the matter is that money rarely stops anyone from getting something they really want. If they want it, they'll find a way, even if it means going into debt.

If they're not spending money with you, it's because someone on your team didn't do a good enough job in justifying why it costs what it does.

That's all we're ever doing in selling.... we're selling the value. How will their life or their business be different as a result of spending that money with you and how certain are they that that will happen?

Why is the thing you're offering, worth the money you're requesting?

No profession or expert on earth is above needing to do this.

Selling doesn't mean being pushy or self-serving or trying to get them to do something they don't want to. The reason we often think that, is because we've experienced terrible salespeople in the past who were like this, and we don't want to be like them, or even be associated with the concept of selling.

Selling means that you're simply going to take the time to help them see what you're offering in a different way than they do, when they say no to you.

Selling is about helping someone to see something through a different lens or from a different perspective, so they can make a better decision for themselves.

Selling is about ethically influencing them to achieve a positive outcome, that they couldn't achieve without you. That's the intervention of selling.

This is why selling is one of the most valuable skills on the planet.

Done correctly, you can help remove the blindfold that was preventing your client from seeing something, just moments earlier. For example, why taking over their full finance function will bring them greater insights, faster AND free them up to work on much higher value activities.

When what we do is helping them to build a more robust, profitable business which can in turn, generate greater wealth for them to live the life that they want.... is there a more valuable skill to have?

The accounting profession is constantly telling you that the path to success is to gain more and more skills, to offer additional services and to use more technology.

And then you do all that and your financial success seems stagnant.

So, you conclude it must be your clients and you invest more time and money into trying to attract better clients.

But still, very little changes so you go back to looking at your service offering and round and around you go. Spending more time and more money and seeing very little results. And by results, I mean more cash in the bank and more time to enjoy it.

But the reality for most accounting businesses, is that within the skills you already have, your standard set of core services and the clients **you're already working with**, there is significantly more impact you can have and much more money to be made, simply by mastering the art of selling.

You can be THE best accountant, bookkeeper or CPA in the world, with ALL the technical skills, but if you can't get people to understand why they need to have monthly management accounts then you're not going to make much impact or much money.

It's only the awarding bodies that sold you your high-priced qualification, that will have you believe this is possible. You're subliminally (or overtly) told that selling is wrong, and you won't need to do it if you're technically superior. You're made to feel that selling is beneath you, which is why they don't train you in how to do it.

So, you leave your training, expecting clients to be throwing money at you for your enhanced skills, only to find that they don't. And at that point, you start to question your skills and ability, which makes you even worse at selling and conclude that you need to be better. You don't. You're more than likely great as you are.

But the training providers will happily sell you your next program to enhance your skills further.

Remember, a best-selling book is not necessarily the best book. It's the book that had the most sales. There are many incredible books that sit on shelves, unheard of, unread and having no impact.

WHAT WE REALISED IN OUR FIRM

All of these excuses I've outlined here, I've witnessed first-hand with the thousands of firms I've worked with over the years and even in our own firm.

Thankfully those days are gone for us, with every team member being actively trained in consultative selling, so that they all feel comfortable in having these types of conversations with clients.

We realised that it's great for Paul – the founder of our firm – to have great sales skills, but he's not the one on the front line dealing with clients on a day-to-day basis, and if he was, he would be the bottleneck in the process.

So instead, we chose to disseminate this valuable skill throughout every team member and to give them the tools and the training, to confidently have sales conversations with clients and to comfortably handle any objections they face.

We figured out how to help clients overcome the uncertainty they have when considering paying significantly higher fees than they've been used to paying.

We learned that uncertainty and scepticism are the *real* barriers to them saying "yes", not time or money. And if you don't have a system to overcome this uncertainty, then they'll never pay your fees, even if they have the time and money to do so.

We realised that it's not about how qualified we are, but about how good we are at communicating what we actually do.

It's not about how many years of experience we have, but how many objections we can confidently overcome.

It's not about how big we are, but how well we deal with clients challenging our prices. The challenging never stops, but if you have the tools and the skills to overcome it, it's not a problem.

Most importantly, we realised that selling shouldn't be something we avoid, but something we should actively be doing for our clients; yes... FOR them.

You want to serve your clients to the best of your ability and to give them the most value you can. But no value can be exchanged unless a sale is made. That is why you need to sell in order to serve.

MORE SKILLS ARE GREAT, BUT...

Developing your skills and learning more ways to deliver greater impact to your clients is a noble thing to do... but... you must first check in with yourself to make sure the skills you currently have are being put to their maximum use.

For years I've seen firms talking about providing advisory services, having been told it's the future to building a successful, profitable firm. That might be the case, but it can't be because the other services and skills you have aren't generating profit and success.

The story I see playing out is a firm not making much money from bookkeeping or compliance services, so they buy into this myth that those services no longer have any value and they're being replaced by technology.

They then invest in training and new tech and more marketing to sell advisory services to their clients, because that's where the gold is, only to find that it isn't.

You see, it was never a problem of bookkeeping and compliance services being unprofitable or dead in the first place. It was a lack of confidence in being able to communicate the full value of those services, charging profitably for them and handling the objections that come back.

They'd believed their clients who told them that they were too expensive, they don't see the value, the other firms are much cheaper, that the software ads all say it's just a click of a button and they could probably do it themselves.

And rather than learn the skills to challenge all of that BS, they accepted it and switched their efforts to making money from a "higher skill", as though they'll be written blank cheques for *those* services and avoid the objections.

But they were wrong, and the same story plays out... too expensive, can't see the value, other firms are cheaper, it's just the click of a button blah de blah de blah.

They have wasted all this time and effort and money in pursuit of something they've already been sitting on.

I'm not saying for a second that developing your skills and offering higher value services isn't a great way to generate more profit and to be more successful... BUT.... It can only happen **once** you've confronted the real issue here, which is the ability to confidently sell the value of bookkeeping, payroll and compliance services and to first maximise their profitability.

If you can't sell those with confidence, the client won't stick around for you to sell advisory services. Why? Because they will lose confidence in YOU.

When you hone the skills to confidently sell what others consider to be a low-level service, you will instill certainty in your clients, and they will be attracted to that and assume that everything else you have to offer will solve their problems too.

More than anything else, people want certainty. Is that what **you're** selling?

STOP SELLING ACCOUNTING SERVICES

(Feel free to switch the word 'accounting' with 'bookkeeping', 'payroll', compliance', 'tax', 'auditing', 'advisory' or anything else.)

You're about to learn that to get better at selling, you have to stop selling accounting services and instead, start selling **certainty.**

Certainty is what we're all after in our lives, and when you give it to your clients, they'll pay whatever price you command.

There's nothing worse than spending money you think is going to be wasted and there's nothing better than spending money and knowing you're going to get exactly what you want.

Your clients want this confidence when they buy from you.

The first thing you're going to have to get comfortable with, is that it's ok to sell what you have, to people who need it. From now on, when you sell, you're not taking money from people – *you're making them feel comfortable about choosing to give it to you.*

Anyone who tells you differently is more concerned with how they appear to their clients, rather than impacting their clients.

So long as you're confident that your skills can solve the problem of the person you're talking to, then sell, sell, sell, knowing that this shows that you care more about helping them that what they might think of you.

I know you may be concerned with what your peers may think of you, but they're more concerned with what *they* lack, than to ever think about you.

And don't worry about what clients think either. If they have a problem with you selling them on what you know they need, then that's their problem, not yours. These people will also have a problem with everything that you do or don't do for them too, so count your blessings when they go elsewhere.

The reality is that people *do* want to speak to someone who can help them to make a decision.

They *do* want to talk to someone who is confident in their ability and who helps *them* to feel confident in the decision they're about to make.

They don't want to talk to someone who looks awkward when the money conversation comes up.

They *don't* want to speak to someone who sells a diluted or discounted version of what they first offered, because this screams uncertainty in how you can help them, what you should charge and ultimately in yourself.

And what they definitely don't want is the pain of their failing business, because no-one has convinced them to invest in its finance function at the level they needed to.

And it's this final reason that should give you the confidence to sell your services with no sense of fear. **You're going to sell the services that you would want, if you were them, knowing what you know,** so that the person you're speaking to never has to live with the consequences that comes with *not* getting the type of great service that I'm sure you provide.

TOTAL CONFIDENCE

By the end of this book, my goal is to give you and your team the confidence, the strategy and the tools you need to be so comfortable with selling your services at the prices you should be charging, so you can live with abundance.

You will start to enjoy selling your services and your clients are going to be happy that you sold them to them, and even happier that they made the decision to buy them from you.

If someone needs to invest ten times more money in the finance function of their business, you're going to look them dead in the eye and explain exactly why your plan is the best option and why they need to reconsider theirs.

This is why I hate the concept of the three-tier pricing methodology that's gained such traction over the years. It abdicates total responsibility for what you know you should do and allows the clients to make the wrong decision (or no decision.)

If someone tells you the price is high, tell them you know and learn to be comfortable with the silence.

If someone tells you they need time to think about it, politely explain that you think that's a mistake, because they've already tried that and it didn't work - the longer this goes on, the more of a mess it will become, the more difficult and costly it will be to fix and all the while, you won't have the information you need to make the decisions you need to make in your business.

You've got to get strong.

You've got to get used to having conversations, which at first, will be uncomfortable. But as you work with them, you'll come to realise that this is exactly what your clients want – someone who is as confident as they'd hope an expert would be, who they're about to trust with their finances.

You can choose that **now** is the time to do this or you can choose to continue to struggle, let everyone walk all over you, feel undervalued, underpaid, overworked and feeling that everyone around you is conspiring against you.

This is about so much more than selling your services.

It's about selling the best staff on why they should join your team.

It's about selling your clients on why they need to complete their tax return this month, rather than in 4 months' time when everyone else does it. Or why they need to move over to this cloud-based software rather than continue with their desktop version.

It's about selling your kids on why they need to go to bed at 8pm rather than at 9pm or why your husband should watch Love Actually rather than Die Hard.

You see, we're always selling, all of the time... or... we're being sold to.

Cracking this will restore the belief in yourself, that you first had when you first chose to do what you're doing now.

If you had the courage to do that, I know I can help you to develop the courage to sell your services with ease and integrity and for much more than you're charging now.

If you're onboard with what I've shared with you so far, keep going. I'm going to unpick a lot of what you've already been taught around selling, remove any limiting beliefs, lay out the proven blueprint for what you need to do and give you the fastest route I know to get you there.

Are you ready?

If so, we're about to get into the common mistakes that firms make when selling, so that you avoid every one of them.

9 REASONS YOU STRUGGLE TO SELL

Anytime you are speaking to a potential client who has concerns about working with you or with an existing client who has questions about taking on that additional service, you're selling. So, whether you realise it or not, like it or not, you're always going to be selling.

Most accounting businesses want those conversations without having to sell. But this isn't an option.

You can call it *selling the value, selling your services or selling yourself*. They're all the same and what you or anyone in your firm is doing, is just making someone feel more comfortable about taking the next step towards buying from you or buying more from you. If you're failing to do that, it could be due to one or more of the following nine reasons:

1. TOO MUCH TALKING. NOT ENOUGH LISTENING

If you want to ethically influence, you must spend more time listening than talking. But people feel most comfortable when they're talking and usually about themselves. Listening moves you into the unknown and what if you can't understand or properly handle what you hear?

If you want to make a great impression and have the best chance of really understanding your client's deepest challenges, you have to listen; actively listen, to every word.

If you talk more than them it's because you want things to go well and you think that talking about you, your firm or how you can help, will put them at ease. But the opposite is true.

When you talk too much, you'll more than likely be trying too hard to sell yourself (as you understand selling to be.) This is a sign of desperately wanting someone to understand things from *your* point of view.

The more you talk, the more you actually give people reasons **not** to buy from you. You invariably find yourself talking your way into objections and out of the sale.

Selling is not about selling yourself. Selling is about listening, ensuring that the client feels understood about their problems and what they want to achieve, and then showing them that you know how to achieve what they want... in as few words as possible.

If you apply the 80:20 rule, they should be speaking for 80% of the time and you for 20%. Aim for that.

Asking better questions is the fastest way to greater sales success.

To help our team to achieve this, we developed a consultative sales framework called The GLOSS Method®.

This guides the questions, develops a deeper understanding of the client's real needs and creates greater certainty that the proposed services will help them achieve their outcome.

This framework also provides the missing agenda to sales meetings and the questions can even be sent ahead of the meeting for the client to prepare.

If you want the **GLOSS Method® PDF** that includes:

- A plug and play consultative sales framework.
- The step-by-step method that unlocks the full opportunity with every client.
- The precise questions to ask at every stage of the process to get the answers you need.

You can download it here – **www.goproposal.com/gloss**

2. LACK OF POSITIONING

Positioning is what makes you different. It's what has people turning up with confidence, ready to buy from you. Properly communicated, it will have them liking you and what you stand for, not what you do.

Most firms do a dreadful job of this, communicating to prospects how friendly or experienced they are, how great their customer service is or how long they've been established. Great, that makes you the same as everyone else, which makes it harder for the client to make a decision.

It's also why you feel you have to price competitively. Why? Because you've just chosen to compete, rather than excel. YOU'VE just made the game harder.

If everyone's the same, the only factor that can be used in making a decision is price, and the cheapest will win.

Firms are reluctant to raise their prices because it's 'their town' or that 'no-one wants to pay higher prices in your area'. But that's not true.

Our firm is in the poor part of a northern, industrial city in the UK. I'm sure other people around us believe that clients won't pay more there, but we charge some of the highest fees in the country. And it's not that we're particularly expensive, we just charge for everything and dare to do so.

Now this is fundamentally a marketing problem, but it just makes selling harder.

Instead of advertising your services or qualifications, use your marketing to position yourself as THE expert.

Provide expert guidance through your videos, special reports and social posts. Better still, write a book on your specialism.

Give all your knowledge away for free. Knowledge has no value anymore, Google put a stop to that, so either I'm going to get the information from you or someone else.

Once you are pre-eminent in the eyes of your dream prospects, people will turn up with fewer objections and be ready to buy from you. When they ask what you charge, they're asking to confirm, having already made up their mind, not as part of their decision-making process. They simply want to know the price, so they can make sure they're giving you the right bank account details with enough money in.

Marketing yourself as the trusted, authoritative accountant is beyond the scope of this book. But it's an important part of the overall sales process. So, I've asked my friends at **The Profitable Firm** to create a really valuable article on this for you. You can read that at www.goproposal.com/trusted

3.WORRY WHAT OTHER FIRMS THINK

You know this prospect is coming from another accountant and you know that accountants talk. So, it's easy to be consumed with what other firms might think of you. It's perfectly natural, especially because you're a 'professional.'

The last thing you want is for other people to label you as a salesperson because that associates you with every bad salesperson out there... and there's a lot of them.

Selling something to someone, who does not need it, especially for your own financial gain, is wrong.

However, selling something to someone who has a problem that you know how to solve, is one of the best things you can do for them.

It's wrong NOT to sell to them and you shouldn't hold off because of what someone might think.

The reality is that they're too consumed with themselves to be thinking about you, and if they do want to take a swipe, it's only through their own inadequacy at what they don't have compared to what you do, so who cares?

4. FEAR OF REJECTION

Selling always exposes you to the chance that someone could say "no" to you and all of the negative feelings that rejection conjures.

I know I have talked about this already, but you see, we all have a deep-rooted desire to be liked and loved and we therefore conclude that's not possible, when people reject us or say "no" to us.

It creates pain. Real pain.

I still remember my first ever girlfriend. We went to the Valentine's ice-skating disco together on our first date. I couldn't skate very well and hung around at the side of the rink. Half-way through the evening, her friend skated over and said you can go now, she's decided to go out with Paul instead. That hurt.

Our lives are layered up with events like that, whether it's your parents' divorce, a partner leaving you or a loved one dying. All of those instill a deep fear of rejection within us and the pain we associate to it.

But one of the reasons we become so fearful of the word "no", is we become so excited and attached to the idea that they might say "yes."

We attach our happiness onto the idea of them saying "yes", and our pain onto the idea of them saying "no." And in those two moves, you're screwed.

Your happiness is now in the hands of others and even with the best sales training in the world, that will always leave you vulnerable.

The quickest way to snap you out of this is to condition yourself so that whether they say "yes" or "no", they both make you feel the same.

To avoid worrying about being rejected, it's not to get too excited when you hear a "yes", or too down on yourself when you hear a "no". You must be neutral.

If they say "yes", sure, that will bring positives, but it will also bring some hardships too.

If they say "no", that may cause some concerns, but it will also create some opportunities.

'Yes' and 'no' are not as opposed as you may think.

If they say "no", you just can't take it personally. You cannot and never will know everything about this person, and if you did, you would fully understand and empathise with why they're saying no. If you've done everything right, their "no" will most definitely be a reflection on them, not you.

Forgive them. Move on.

I know this is easier to say than do, especially if you are struggling financially, because you pin all of your hopes on this one client saying "yes." But with the new strategy and mindset you're going to have, you'll be far more persistent, relentless and successful in your pursuit of your goals.

You want them to say "yes" for *their* sake, not yours.

Some will. Some won't. So what? Someone's waiting.

You will go again with renewed confidence.

You will stop thinking it's about your skill level or what you charge.

You will not let this dent your confidence.

You will learn to ask the question that will help them to overcome their insecurities about you or your price.

5. NEVER SHOWN HOW TO SELL

Everyone is born a great salesperson.

As a child you were a master of persuasion.

When my kids go to bed, they will shout down for a hug, which I can't resist.

When I'm in their room, they will then try to upsell me on reading them a story. If I agree, then they'll want another, then a drink, then a biscuit, then their TV on for 10 more minutes. If I say no, they will ask if they can read some more, because they know they're more likely to get a yes to that.

When they hear me say no, they keep their eyes on the prize, which is to stay up longer, and keep going.

I was cooking dinner once and getting close to serving it up.

My 10-year-old son – Leo - asked me to come and watch a YouTube clip.

I said, "No. I can't, I'm about to serve dinner." (A very clear 'no.')

He said, "How long will that take?" (Not interested in my 'no'.)

"Ten minutes" I said. (A very clear objection to any impending request.)

"But this will only take ten seconds." He said.

SOLD.

Kids don't care. They keep going and I harness that ability in my children.

But most kids get shouted at and trained out of selling, and then have to be retrained back into it at a later date.

And that retraining either never happens or is done by people who don't understand what selling really is, scarring you mentally for life.

Within the accounting space, I have seen selling being trained in THE most manipulative sense imaginable. I remember going on one 'sales training webinar', where the 'expert' explained that selling was "establishing your client's maximum willingness to pay, and then to use a variety of psychological techniques to get them to pay as close to that amount as possible."

Your client's maximum willingness to pay has got nothing to do with you. Maybe they should spend much less than that. Maybe they should spend much more. If that's your guiding star, you will end up in totally the wrong place for you and them.

So, you must be very guarded with any sales training you receive.

I always think that the ultimate test of the ethics of your sales process is – would you use them on your best friend, and then, would you be happy to tell them about the process you used?

Selling is something you need to train yourself in. You need to commit time to it and so do your team.

You need to role play scenarios and get comfortable with feeling uncomfortable.

I'm a 2nd Dan Black Belt in a Combat Ju-Jitsu. We would train hard so that if we were ever in a fight, it would be easy.

But don't beat yourself up at this point. If you're not all that good at it, well done for picking up this book to learn how to do it right.

TOP TIP: Role playing is always going to feel embarrassing initially, but it's so valuable. And if feeling embarrassed, stops you from doing it, you've got to ask yourself, "Is me feeling slightly embarrassed in front of my team, more important than serving our clients to a higher level and making more money?"

Is it?

One of the best training sessions I ever saw was in a Physiotherapist practice, for how to offer a customer a cup of coffee. They always say no to it you see, and the theory was if we can't sell them on the idea of having a coffee, what chance do we have on selling them on a 12-week care plan.

So, one by one the staff took it in turns to come in and had to say "no" to the coffee initially. The person taking the turn of the receptionist had to handle the objections.

Receptionist: Can I get you a coffee?

Customer: No thanks, I've just had one. (They've always just had one by the way.)

Receptionist: It's not a problem, I'm making one myself.

Customer: It's ok thank you.

Receptionist: We serve the best coffee in town, let me show you the menu. (Yes, they had a menu.)

Customer: (silence)

Receptionist: AND... I'm about to open a packet of chocolate HobNob biscuits.

Customer: OK then.

The receptionist had to then come from behind reception and sit with the customer, talk to them, relax them and have a coffee with them.

They would train different scenarios for 2 hours every single week. If you were their competitor, what chance would you have against them, when they're evolving consistently every single week, year in, year out.

In order for you to operate at this level, you need to start by setting a training plan in the diary, every week.

For the next six weeks you could get everyone on your team to read this book. Each week they come to a one-hour training session where you simply take a section off the book at a time, review it, discuss the parts you like, challenge the parts you don't and agree what actions you're going to take.

For the six weeks after that, you can act out scenarios in groups based on the **"The 6 Common Objections to Your Services"** (a chapter in this book.)

You create a fictional client and present a legitimate set of services to them. The client gives one of the objections and using the lessons in this book and your own experience, you explore ways to handle it. You can have fun with it. Swear if that's realistic.

If the first time you hear an F-bomb dropped is in a client meeting, it will completely throw you off your game. Use them in your training sessions if need be. Train harder than you need to so that the real-life situation will be easy.

If you did the training session over Zoom, you can record it and use it as a resource in the future for the best way to handle these scenarios.

There's your training plan for the next 12 weeks.

6. NO UNDERSTANDING OF WHY PEOPLE OBJECT

Closely tied to no sales training, is no understanding of why people *really* object.

If you think it's only because of price, with respect, you're mistaken. Society, the news, media, would have you believe that no-one has any money, but this just isn't true.

I'm from a large mining village in the north of England. The mine once provided the majority of the village's employment and closed down in 2007, leaving little work opportunity for a large number of its inhabitants. The local economy has since been supported with call centres being located nearby and a large Amazon warehouse. But I promise, if I was to return there and walk around, I would **not** see people wearing the cheapest clothes, driving the cheapest cars or not going on holiday.

Yes, there are some people who can't pay your fees, but far fewer than you think. But because we hear them say things like "That's too expensive," "That's more than I'm willing to pay," or "I don't see the value in paying that." we conclude that their objection has something to do with money, when it probably doesn't.

The majority of people will be objecting to something else, but they just don't know how to communicate that to you, so money is the easiest excuse to sell you, and you buy it.

Remember, a sale is always being made and you're either selling, or your being sold to.

They're objecting for so many other reasons, some of which they don't even know themselves. The **'objections'** chapter is coming up which goes into great depth on this and I recommend you read it like your business depends upon it... because it probably does.

Just know for now that what people say, they don't necessarily mean. Our job is to unearth that true meaning. It's not their job to reveal it to us.

I have had so many accountants and bookkeepers come to me saying their clients can't afford it and they want a discount or they're going somewhere else. I have given them **one line** to say and they always come back to me saying the same thing "You'll never guess what? They signed up at the full price!"

Now they can only use that line because they've followed this sales process up to that point, and the discount question is their last attempt at an objection.

The price wasn't lowered, they didn't go anywhere else, they didn't win the lottery. They miraculously found the money and signed-up.

To learn my response to the **"Can we have a discount?"** question, visit **www.goproposal.com/discount** and watch the video or scan the following QR Code on your phone...

7. NO SALES SYSTEM

Learning the correct response to objections like "Can we have a discount?" is super useful, but it's just a tactic.

Tactics are the building blocks of **strategies**, and strategies, processes, philosophies and software are the building blocks of **systems.**

Learning one clever line is never going to make a huge difference.

Putting the correct systems in place that consider every touch point a client has with you, from their first contact, right the way through to signing up with you and then buying more from you, will make a huge difference.

Creating a repeatable, manageable process that everyone on your team can buy into, where there are no cracks, where software does the heavy lifting, that is governed by strong philosophies, that people are trained in, that is constantly evolving, where there are no bottlenecks, that you can trust to deliver predictable results... that's a system, that's where you win.

All of these things (and more) are what goes into a sales system and each can be optimised in their own right.

It will be the most impactful thing you can do in your business to boost your profits.

If you're an army of one or just started out, it's how you get away from having to do all the selling.

If you have a team of people, this is how you will get the most from the investment you're making in those people.

When I first met Paul, I asked "Why are you doing the selling, when we can build a system and have 13 members of staff doing the selling instead?"

You might not have thought about it, but you do already have a sales system. It just might not be a very good one.

Building a system with 10 touch points, each of which can be made 10% better, compounds and creates stunning results.

Nothing is ever perfect when they start, especially systems. But if you want them to be great, you have to get comfortable with them first being average, then good and THEN great.

This is not about perfection, it's about progress.

We have to start, then fix, then improve. But the key part here is we **have to start.**

8. YOU KNOW THEM

Knowing someone personally can be a real challenge when it comes to selling to them.

Whether it's a family member, a friend, a friend of a friend, someone you play golf with, a parent at your children's school or even a referral from any of those people.

Everything I've explained about your fear of judgement and not wanting to be seen as 'greedy' or 'salesy' is massively heightened, because you think they'll be telling everyone you know.

So, you either avoid selling to this group of people, which forces you to reject a large number of potential clients (everyone you know or knows the people you know.)

Or you take them on and do the worst thing possible for this type of relationship in particular… you give them a discount. Because it's not just you who feels uncomfortable in this situation!

So, let me explain how you can still sell to these people, avoid losing money, and still feel totally comfortable.

Whether you are able to make these relationships a success or not, all comes down to how it starts.

The five words I'm about to teach you will ensure it starts off on the right footing. They just need to be learned, practiced and forever be your trigger point for what comes next.

So, let's describe a situation. A family member calls you up and explains that their friend needs an accountant and would you speak to them. They finish the call with "I've told them you'll look after them."

This, as we all know, is code for 'do it cheaply.' This adds that extra level of guilt, awkwardness and a sense of obligation on the following call.

You say, "Sure." You call the friend and say, "Hey, John's told me to give you a call. He said you were in need of an accountant and that you're his friend. Well, I'd love to help you, come down and see us." Or something to that effect.

And in that one seemingly innocent interaction, you doomed the relationship. Why? Because you failed to assume the position of the authoritative, professional expert in their mind… and yours.

They will now turn up, perhaps expecting to get 'mate's rates', and if they don't, you will certainly be expecting to give them. So, let's change the whole tone with five words.

You call the friend "Hey, John's told me to give you a call. He said you were in need of an accountant and that you're his friend. Well, I'd love to help you, come down and see us. But… **I need you to know**…"

And there it is. In those five words, you just became important in their mind and they (just like you are now) are waiting with eager anticipation to hear what comes next, sensing the weight of what's to follow.

"… **I need you to know**… when you walk in my door, I'm a fully qualified chartered accountant who does x, y and z. I will speak to you in the exact same way I speak to all my other clients. You will be given the same advice, the same levels of respect, service and time and for that, you will need to pay the same money. Is that ok?"

And here's the best part… they would rather you do that, because - and this is going to totally fry your mind - you think *you're the only one* feeling uncomfortable in this relationship, when it comes to money or telling them what to do; but you're not.

They are feeling *equally* uncomfortable and worried about what they'll have to pay, whether they'll get the same level of service and how this will all work. They'll be so glad you brought this up.

When you stop to think about it, you're wracked with fear, guilt and anxiety about what this person is thinking and how this relationship will work. But… they're thinking exactly the same. It's crazy.

You can cut through all of that tiring nonsense with one, simple, honest conversation.

Remind yourself of what your family member said, "I've told them you'll look after them."

What I've described above is actually the only way you *can* successfully do that and everyone – your family member, their friend, your team and yourself – will thank you for this.

And if, when you tell them this, they say they were just looking for a cheap discounted service, you can politely explain that that's not what you do and put them in touch with someone else.

It's better to have that slightly tricky conversation then, rather than when it all blows up in 12 months' time.

Is all of this hard to do? **YES.**

Is it hard to take on this person for a low rate, with a high sense of obligation, knowing you can never serve them for that and that ultimately the relationship will fail, because you and your team will end up hating them and they'll never feel comfortable asking for anything extra or being critical if anything ever goes wrong? **YES.**

They're both hard. **Choose your hard.**

9. YOU HAVE A WEAKNESS SOMEWHERE ELSE

I was hesitant to put this one in, because I don't want to add doubt to your mind or give you any unnecessary excuses.

But something that *could* be affecting your ability to sell is that you have a weakness in another part of your business.

So, let's say you know that your onboarding system sucks or there's a problem with the delivery system which means it's a struggle to get tax returns completed on time. This can make it very hard to be enthusiastically authentic when you're selling; certainly not at the required level to do a solid job of it.

And all the sales training in the world won't fix it, because the real issue lies somewhere else.

Now that said, and the reason for my hesitation, is that maybe it *is* good enough and you just don't know it. Or maybe it's nearly there and with just a day or two's effort from you and the team, you could get it to a point where you *would* be happy with it.

I just know what you guys are like... you want everything to be perfect. And why do you strive for that? Because that's what you're trained to do and what makes you a great accountant, bookkeeper or CPA. Making a set of financials as close to perfect as possible is your job and your natural proclivity. It's what makes you great at your craft.

But when it comes to processes and systems, they will never be perfect.

So, you need to bring some real self-awareness to this point.

The underlying reason why we aim for perfection is to avoid judgement. Judgement from who? Who are you *really* afraid of failing in front of?

Or is it actually good enough and you just *think* it could be better, but you need to accept where it is? It's ok. Move on.

Is it not *quite* good enough, but you're avoiding pushing it over the line for fear that you will then have to sell it?

Is it that you have a member of staff who just can't deliver who needs to be trained or moved on, but you don't feel comfortable having that conversation?

Or is it actually bad and it needs work?

Whatever the case, I just want you to ask yourself these three questions...

1. Is there a part of our onboarding system, delivery system or team that is affecting my ability to sell?
2. What big change would need to happen, to make me ridiculously enthusiastic about selling?
3. What small change could we make this week, that would give me enough confidence, for this not to affect my ability to sell?

I would then challenge you to set the time aside... right now... just book the time in your diary to start this ball rolling to get this fixed.

That might mean setting up practice management software like **Senta** and locking down version one of your onboarding system, for example. That's it; that would be totally doable if you focussed on it.

I was once working ridiculously hard in my business and someone called me lazy. I said, "What do you mean lazy? I'm the hardest worker there is!"

He said, "You're lazy because you're avoiding the one thing you know you should do, which is to sell. But through fear, you're putting it off and busying yourself elsewhere."

This fear can be:

- ☐ Fear of correcting something and getting it wrong, which means you will be judged.
- ☐ Fear of correcting something and getting it right, which then means you have to sell it, which puts you back in the firing line for judgment.
- ☐ Fear of having to ignore other responsibilities while you fix this thing, and what people will think of you.

When I did the rewrite of this book, I had to go into dark mode. I had to ignore the phone, ignore emails, clients, staff and even ignore my wife.

But if I didn't do that, I would not have got this finished. I wrote 27,000 words in a little over a week.

Most people aren't prepared to deal with the fallout that comes from committing to something so fully and so intensely. But it's that level of effort that's required to get things to the point where you can hit publish, send, go live, launch.

My point is, whatever you feel is broken that is restricting your ability to sell, most things can be fixed with one week's worth of relentless, selfish, my-life-depends-on-this level of commitment, or certainly taken to a point where it's no longer a problem.

So if there is something that needs your attention, fix it; fix it now. Just make sure it's not an excuse to be lazy a.k.a. avoiding the one thing you know you should be doing, which is to SELL.

WHY YOU JUST NEED TO BE YOU

If I was visiting your town for the night and I got in touch with you to ask where I should eat, what would you say? And more importantly, **how** would you respond?

Just think about it for a second. Think how you've sold your favourite restaurant to others.

If you asked me, I'd say "You've GOT to go to the Three Acres. The food is gorgeous. Everything is locally sourced and cooked fresh. They do these scallops with gruyere cheese as a starter, which are to die for. The fillet steak is divine or the cod or any of the main courses to be fair, and you get loads. They do an assiette of desserts that give you a taste of all their best ones. All the local celebrities go there, and you can see their pictures on the wall. Make sure you book in advance because they get booked up. Check out their reviews on Trip Advisor. "

I would really go to town on you. I'd be showing you pictures, pulling up the menu, hell, I'd even go with you.

I would do my best to transfer my energy and enthusiasm over to you and I wouldn't feel any fear or anxiety at all. I would be excited for you. I would feel great and more importantly, I would want you to feel great, by going.

Now you would never consider this to be selling. I am simply influencing you towards doing something I know is going to enhance your life.

If only you would speak to your clients with this same energy, all of your sales problems or fears would disappear.

Selling isn't difficult or bad. We do it all day, every day with our family and friends. We do it with passion and no fear. In fact, it feels very natural.

So why doesn't this happen naturally in your firm?

The answer is simple to explain.

When you get to work, you start acting and behaving differently, *because* you're at work.

You start to gravitate towards something that actually feels very unnatural. Have you noticed this yourself? When you're talking to a client, all of a sudden you start talking differently to how you talk to your friends?

The more interesting question, is why?

The only answer I ever hear is "Because that's what everyone else does." That's it.

We fall into this mode of talking differently, dressing differently, acting differently, just because that's what we've seen everyone else do.

I think they call it "being professional."

You're told to act professionally at work, but then no-one tells you what that really means. I don't know either, but I'm sure it's not to act like somebody you're not.

You fundamentally change the way you are, to gain the approval of your team and your clients. And there starts the problem. You are now someone you're not and therefore find it difficult to do something that should come natural to you – sell.

For you to become the best you can be at selling, you simply have to become the best version of yourself, not a half-baked, diluted, professional version of what you *think* you should be.

When people become more concerned with how they are perceived, rather than how they can serve, they can never be their best self; they can never have the right level of energy to transfer to a client, and that's all a sale is – a transfer of energy.

When you focus on you, the energy goes inward.

When you focus on them, it goes out.

And energy, like time, is finite. You only get so much and must protect it fiercely. You must become acutely aware of where and how it's being channelled. (I told you we'd be going deep.)

To become the best salesperson you can ever be, you just have to be you.

You have to uncouple yourself from the version of you, you think you have to be at work and just be you.

I cannot tell you the number of times I have simply given permission to 'professional' people to just be themselves and to do what is naturally in their heart.

And now I'm giving you permission to do the same.

Be the best version of *you*, that *you* can be.

Talk and communicate with your clients in a way that people who love you, *love you to do*, and watch the difference it makes.

Your friends and family love you because you are you. And the reason it's easy at home is because you don't care what they think of you; you know you're not being judged so you feel more confident to be you.

You are enough.

If your clients don't like you for being you, then they're not for you and that's fine.

What we're all craving for is people just to be their authentic selves, warts and all.

How annoying is it when you hear politicians avoiding questions or lying to cover up a mistake?

Wouldn't you be more endeared to them if they just said, "We've made a mistake here, really sorry, we're humans doing our best, we messed up and this is what we're going to do to put it right."

Wouldn't that be so refreshing? Wouldn't you trust them so much more?

By being your authentic self, the client will naturally trust you so much more because they will believe *fully*, in the version of you that you're presenting them with.

If you present a façade, they will see through it and smell it a mile off.

So, the one thing you need your clients to have is total trust in you, because they need to be able to trust themselves to make the right decision with certainty. But how can they ever have that trust, when what you're presenting them with is, and I say this with the greatest of respect, a lie.

The litmus test is - if your best friend heard you talking to a client in the way you normally talk to them, would they think you were being authentic or .... weird? And the next question to ask is, if they had only ever seen that side of you, would they still want to be your best friend?

You are not selling services; you are changing people's lives. Never forget that.

The way that you get to do that is through the way that you make people feel by doing business with you, not just what you do in reconciling their accounts or filing a tax return.

People will forget what you say and forget what you do, but they will never forget how you make them *feel*.

What people really want from you is an energy and a certainty that they perceive they lack in themselves. They are drawn to it like a magnet.

I bet the reason you follow the people you do on social media is because you believe they have something that you want; that you lack. By connecting with them, you feel closer towards the thing that you want.

When you're able to change the way people feel when they're around you, you will never have to worry about selling ever again. When this happens, people want to buy from you and will be asking what else you have to sell to them.

They will buy into your energy and into what you can really do for them – *which is to change their lives.*

Knowing this, I want you to be careful of where you lose your energy.

Become very aware of the people who take your energy from you and either remove them from your life, or if you can't, develop ways to better manage your interactions with them.

Become very aware of what information you consume and from where. If you go to bed at night having just listened to the news, or wake up and put it on, stop it. I haven't listened to the news for over ten years and my children don't even know what it is.

Become very aware of your negative inner voice and what it's saying to you. Just listen to it. It's not you. It's talking to you and trying to convince you that it is, but it's not. Just listen to it and it will go quiet.

Learn to be you.

You are enough as you are.

Only you can do you, so do you; not a diluted version of you.

Be you and let your energy shine.

Never let anyone take your energy without your permission.

It's more valuable than money. But you don't treat it like it is.

The irony here is that energy is finite, money is not. It's the transfer of energy that makes the sale that will bring money to you. So if you let your energy be wasted, you won't have enough in the bank to transfer, in order to make the sale and get the cash.

Protect your energy more than you protect your money, and the greatest protection you can give your energy is to just be you... it's enough.

You're enough.

4 REASONS WHY CLIENTS REALLY SAY "NO"

The real reason clients say 'no' to working with you or to buying more from you, is a lack of trust. A lack of trust makes their decision to invest with you feel risky, so they'll tell you it's down to time or money.

They'll say, "It's too expensive" or "You're charging way more than my previous accountant." But they're only saying that to protect themselves from what they perceive to be a bad decision.

What's interesting here, is what they lack trust in, and there are four key areas of mistrust.

1. LACK OF TRUST IN THEMSELVES

Before reading this book, most people think that it's high prices that cause a client to say "no". So they look to what other firms charge and try to replicate *their* low fees so as to avoid rejection. But they don't stop to think that the root cause of mistrust has nothing to do with them or their prices.

The No.1 reason the clients say "no", regardless of what excuse they give you, is that **they don't trust themselves.**

They've made mistakes before and they don't want to repeat that. They've made so many bad decisions in the past, that they doubt they can ever make a good one again.

They bought a car and the engine needed replacing. They booked a holiday and the hotel was next to a building site. They married the wrong brother. They sold their shares when they should have held on. Whatever. They've made mistakes and don't want to make another.

It's not that they don't trust you, but likewise, you've done nothing to encourage a sense of trust in you either. So, you're not to blame for this mistrust, but you kind of are. We'll get onto that.

Making decisions is the power that moves businesses and lives forward. If no decision is ever made, nothing progresses. But decision making takes practice to keep the ability alive.

People can lose their ability to make decisions and the longer that carries on, the worse it gets.

2. A LACK OF TRUST IN YOU

If it's not a lack of trust in themselves, it will likely be a lack of trust in you. This is not to be taken personally. People are naturally wary about parting with cash, entering into relationships and signing contracts and that's fine. In fact, it's natural.

There are ways you can build trust, but sometimes, the only thing that will transition them from distrusting you to trusting you, is time.

Sometimes we have to be patient and play the long game and too many firms throw the towel in when they get knocked back. Dig in. When this client eventually signs up, it will be for high monthly fees for the next ten years. What would that equate to? Is that not worth being patient for?

Outside of the accounting industry, the largest annual contract a client of mine landed was for £5m a year. It took them over ten years to build the trust required to reel them in. That contract turned into £10m over the next two years. That was where I first learned about patience in business.

In my personal life, it took my wife 15 years to agree to go out with me, and when she did, she agreed to marry me in the same breath.

What most firms do is buy into the money myth they hear from their clients and lower their prices as a result. This forces them to spend less time with prospects because they're not able to commit to investing in that relationship for any length of time. So, they're forever playing a short game for small wins.

But if you accounted for that level of investment in the fees you charged, you could afford to devote the time required to build the trust they need, to take them to the point where they would willingly pay top dollar.

Most firms would never dream of committing that level of resource to nurturing those relationships. They couldn't do it because they don't have the staff, and they don't have the staff because they don't have the money to hire them and train them. Why? Because they don't charge the fees that would generate the profit required. And round and around they go, blaming clients, fixing surface problems and staying frustrated.

It's never been about whether *they* can afford you. It's always been about the time you can afford *them.*

Once you're able to give them the time they need to build the trust, it's part 'what you say' and the questions you ask in that time, but also, 'how you act.'

Only 7% of how you communicate with clients comes from the words you say. The rest is gleaned from the way you sit, the way you greet them, your eye contact and your tone of voice.

All of these factors and more are being considered when people are deciding whether to trust you or not, even down to the little words you say.

I know of an estate agent who was losing sales and being aggressively knocked down on his fee. He recorded his sales calls and when he played them back, it was all down to one word he was saying. When clients asked him what the fee was, he was saying "I *usually* charge…" Usually!

What do you think when you hear that word? "Well, what are you going to charge me?" He intentionally removed that one word from his conversations and his sales soared.

Do you look, sound and act like someone I should trust to invest my money into and build a long-term relationship with?

With more and more of these types of client interactions moving onto Zoom meetings and the like, it's never been easier to record yourself and watch yourself back.

It can be a tough watch, but you need to know whether you would buy from you.

3. LACK OF TRUST BECAUSE YOU'RE TOO CHEAP

Being too cheap can cause real distrust. A client will never tell you that, but low fees can corrode their trust when they're preparing to make a decision.

When you're looking for a plumber or an electrician to work on your house, are you looking for the cheapest? Is that what you'd Google? Cheapest plumber.

If you were to get a plumber and they offered you a really low price, would you be concerned? Would you be worried about how good they were, the quality of the materials they use and that if there was ever a problem, would they come back to fix it?

We bought a washing machine recently and we expected to pay around £500 for one. But then we saw one at £700 and it made us start to question what the £500 ones were lacking.

The price changes the way you feel about something. Subconsciously we become less trusting of the cheaper options and more trusting of the more expensive ones.

Price is a statement of value and high fees are a legitimate way of differentiating yourself from your competitors.

If you genuinely believe that you're great at what you do, better than all of the others out there, care more than anyone else, prepared to go above and beyond, but you charge low fees, there is clearly a disconnect between what you believe and your reality. This doubt will be felt by your clients. They won't believe your promises and will feel that it's too good to be true.

If you want to stack 'em high and sell 'em cheap, fine. If you expect every service to run perfectly smoothly, no clients to ever cause you an issue, where everything is given to you on time, all your staff are happy to be paid low fees and work to impeccable standards and there's never going to be a global pandemic that makes clients infinitely more demanding overnight, where rules and regulations change on a weekly basis, then cool, charge those low fees.

I don't know where your fees are right now, but I'd guess they're lower than they could be.

Before the Corona virus hit, I knew of firms who were selling payroll services as a loss leader to bring clients in *and* because they didn't think it was a valued service. They were selling compliance services at more or less break even because they'd been sold on the idea that compliance was dead. And they made their money by selling advisory services for higher fees. And there were some large firms doing this.

Then Covid hit and what happened? Clients scaled back advisory services, needed extra support with their compliance obligations and a ridiculous level of support to help them understand government schemes to help them pay their staff.

In the UK, people had lived for decades without ever uttering the word 'furlough' and now it was used in every other sentence.

Literally overnight, the tables turned. The services they'd relied upon to generate profit disappeared and the services that made little or no money required an investment of time that their profit margins just couldn't support.

I know of firms who had to lay off staff or go into complete lockdown, turning off their emails and phones because they couldn't cope.

And those firms blamed the pandemic for their situation.

Bullshit.

Storms come; it's the only thing that's guaranteed in business, it's the path of the entrepreneur.

Clients complain and sue you.

Governing bodies fine you.

Clients try to get you down on price.

Competitors try to steal your business.

Technology undermines your value.

Legislation changes.

Staff make mistakes.

Staff leave.

Clients leave.

Recessions hit.

Pandemics hit.

Shit happens.

Storms come and you need to have a business and a pricing model that survives storms, because if you don't, when they come, and they will come, you will be blown all over the place.

Pricing low doesn't just create doubt and mistrust, it is downright dangerous.

If you ever win business because you were cheap, see that as a red flag and know you've just moved into the danger zone.

"Yeah, but we have to have low prices to get our foot in the door because we've just started, we're only small, we don't have the same qualifications as the others, we're *just* bookkeepers, we're just this, we're just that, we're only…"

I remember a start-up, army of one, accountancy business from Wales, message me. I distinctly remember it because I was in Starbucks in San Jose at the time.

He said, "I've just started a free trial of GoProposal and I love the philosophies but I'm only just starting out, clients won't pay those types of fees and I'm not sure I can really afford to pay the subscription cost."

I called him and described the journey he was about to go on and where he would end up… with a load of clients, paying ridiculously low fees, who he would begrudge serving and he would struggle to ever raise their prices in the future. I explained that he had a chance to get this right from the get-go. That he had this one unique opportunity to start out doing this right. Yes, it would be hard, but not as hard as the alternative. I explained how he couldn't afford NOT to invest in the product because if it enabled him to charge 50% more than he would have done without it, then within just a few clients it would be paying for itself and making him money.

On that call I described a unique observation I'd made some years before... **the way you buy, is the way you sell.**

Let me explain what I mean.

Several years ago, I was doing some sales training with two members of staff in an ecommerce business. Both received the same training and seemed equally enthused to implement what I'd taught them.

A few months later I returned and one of them was absolutely flying and the other was still struggling and I couldn't understand why.

After some probing, I hit on a unique discovery, which was how they bought products themselves.

The first one was happy to buy things and if it wasn't right, return them.

The second one was very cautious and would always go home and think about things.

So how did the sales conversations go?

The first one would say to clients, "Look, just buy it, and if you don't like it, you can always send it back. We have a 250 day returns policy and we'll pay for the return postage."

The second one would say, "Look, don't feel that you have to rush into the decision now, take your time, have a think about it and come back to me if you're interested."

You see, we don't see the world as it is, we see the world *as we are.*

We project our own fears and doubts onto the world and onto our clients.

If the accountant from Wales was looking at GoProposal as a cost rather than an investment and thinking it was too expensive, what was he projecting onto his clients about *his* services? Exactly: as a cost.

If you want to change the way that people perceive you, you've got to change the way that you perceive the world.

If you want people to change the way they act with you, you've got to become very aware of how you act with the world, because whether you know it or not, like it or not, you will be projecting your own thoughts about the world onto your clients and *it will change them.*

If you're mistrusting, they will be distrusting of you.

If you see everything as a cost, *they* will see everything as a cost.

The best salespeople are the best buyers.

I'm a salesperson's dream. I walk into the Apple shop and say, "Right, I want the biggest iPhone you've got with the largest memory, the best case and when you've sold me that, sell me the insurance, the iPods, the lot. Let's go."

One year after signing up with us, the Welsh accountant called me on my mobile to thank me. He'd just landed his first £1k+ per month client. He was still an army of one and this was a great achievement.

If he'd have started out trying to win clients by being cheap, who knows what would have happened to him.

4. LACK OF TRUST IN THE OUTCOME

A big thing that affects your client's trust, is whether they will get the outcome they want.

Now the outcome is not the delivery of the service you provide. The outcome is what they achieve as a *result* of the service you provide.

This throws up our first problem. Do you know what outcomes your clients want?

Let me give you an example. When I set up my business, I had three clear goals – for us to move into a house closer to our children's school, for my wife to have the option to leave work if she wanted to and to walk my children to and from school each day.

With respect, I don't care about the bookkeeping service you provide me with. I do care about whether I can get my kids from school on a Friday, rather than scrambling around for receipts and generating invoices.

I don't care about the financial forecast. I do care that if we hit it, then Bekki can hand her notice in at work.

But if you don't know the outcome I'm looking for, how on earth can you instil the trust that you can help me to achieve that outcome?

If every time we speak on the phone, you're not asking me "Has Bekki handed her notice in yet? Have you bought that house yet? Is there anything we can be doing to get you there faster?" Then just know that you can't possibly be giving me all the value that you can.

So, the first question is, do you have a sales process that uncovers the outcomes and do all of your staff know about them?

When I made MAP aware of this concept, we started including client's outcomes on the first page of management reports, as a reminder of why we're doing what we're doing.

So, step one is to identify the outcomes.

Step two is to provide realistic and honest assurances about how you're going to help them get there. You don't have to promise the earth and in fact, people will have more trust in the outcome if you tell them where things are likely to go wrong as well.

It's ok to say to a client "Look, the first thing we need to do is transfer you from your desktop accounting package over to Xero. As we do this, there will be a clean-up exercise which tends to cause some frustrations, but don't worry, we'll do a full cross-check to ensure there is no loss of data using our 30-point checklist, that gets signed off by a senior accountant before we turn your old system off. We will then start to train you in your new system which we do over 3 x 45minute sessions. During these, I guarantee at least one member of your team, or maybe you, will hate us and think you've made the wrong choice in switching systems. This is perfectly natural when you're learning new software. Don't worry, we've got video training, a cheat-sheet help guide and our support package to help you with any initial frustrations. I promise that by month 3, everyone will love the fact that you've moved over, because of what it will make possible for you."

Mapping out the client's onboarding journey, calling out potential bumps in the road up front, having checklists, sign-off processes and realistic timeframes, all of these things help to provide certainty in the outcome.

During proposal meetings at MAP, we hand clients our onboarding brochure. This starts to give them certainty in what will happen next. This is a physical, well designed, high quality brochure, which in itself gives certainty.

Last year my wife had her eyebrows microbladed (tattooed on). **Before** she scheduled her appointment, she was given a guide about the range of emotions she would go through after she'd had them done. Even though not all of those emotions were positive, they provided certainty, which is all anyone is looking for from you.

But what if they've been promised certainty in the past and had been let down by a previous firm. Just giving them certainty in you won't heal the damage the other firm has caused, because that firm likely said the same thing to them too.

Firstly, never bad-mouth their previous accountant or the software they're using, because all you're doing is reinforcing distrust in their own ability to make a decision.

Instead, restore their confidence in themselves. "I know you didn't get the outcome you were looking for last time, but it's great that you recognised that, because most businesses don't and just struggle on. You know what you want and now we know what doesn't work, so it's going to be easier and faster for us to get you to the results that you *do* want."

Make them feel good about what they did in the past by congratulating them for the positive decisions they have made. Don't scald them for using desktop software, instead, say "Well done for using software, some people still use spreadsheets. So well done for making that decision. Now, based on the outcomes you're looking to achieve, you need to be on the cloud and here's why..."

This then perfectly tees you up to discuss the certainty you can provide them in the next decision they're about to make.

However, when you're talking to a prospect about how their previous firm failed to help them achieve their outcome, you've got to be prepared to identify if the *client* contributed to those failed outcomes.

For example, it could be the case that they massively underinvested into the finance function or they attempted to do the bookkeeping themselves which led to all the challenges. So, you have to be prepared to be very frank with the client, point out any obvious failings and be prepared to stand up for what you know to be right.

Let's say they come to you and want monthly Management Accounts. They were annoyed with their previous firm, because they took 20 days after month end to complete, but they needed them completed within 7 days, ready for their board meeting.

You then give them assurances that with your process, you can achieve that.

But they then tell you that they want to do their own bookkeeping. You take a look in their accounting software and realise it's all over the place.

You then explain that you can't possibly achieve that deadline unless they let you do the bookkeeping too, and they would need to be on your daily reconciliation package for you to stand a chance of hitting their deadline.

They then tell you that they don't want to spend that much and would prefer to keep it in-house and instead, request some bookkeeping training from you.

At that point, you've got to be prepared to say, "With respect, bookkeeping is a highly skilled function when done properly. While we *could* train you in it, we will never be able to get you to the standard that my team operates at, and respectfully, we will be forever cleaning up your mistakes. You've told me that you were frustrated with your previous accountant because they couldn't give you the management report you needed, in time for your board meeting, for you to make important decisions about the direction of your business. I'm saying that we definitely can, but only if you're prepared to stop doing the bookkeeping yourself and are willing to invest quite a bit more for us to handle this for you. Your old accountant had no chance of ever being able to deliver these results, based on what they were offering and what they were charging. We can, but it has to be done our way and for this fee. **Is having that**

management report on time, important enough for you to let go of doing the bookkeeping yourself and for you to start paying this amount?"

That's the question to ask. Build the case, present the facts, ask the question with total confidence, then shut up.

Healing distrust caused by others can only be done if you are in full awareness of the facts and are prepared to have this tough conversation.

Having conversations like this is hard. *Not* having conversations like this is hard. Choose your hard.

I know I'm sharing lots of ways to handle objections and strategies and scripts for having difficult conversations. This gives you comfort knowing you have a resource you can rely upon, but it also a sense of overwhelm, because how the hell are you and your team going to remember them all? The answer is **with continual practice and training.** Get your entire team to read this book. Get them the Audible version if they prefer. Then schedule a review session where you can all sit down and share your learnings. Then regular training sessions. Weekly at first, then monthly. Go over and over them. Role play. Have fun. There is nothing here that isn't totally ethical and well within your ability to learn and deliver with confidence. It will just require practice. But you have to commit the time, or nothing will change.

6 COMMON OBJECTIONS TO YOUR SERVICES

When someone tells you they were late to the meeting because of traffic problems, that's an excuse. What they really mean is that they didn't leave the house on time and didn't account for the extra traffic at that time.

When someone says they don't have time to exercise, what they really mean is that they've prioritised watching the latest boxset on Netflix.

When my son says he's not dressed for school because he can't find his uniform, what he really means is that he's been too busy playing Roblox with his friends to bother looking for it.

What people say and what they mean are two different things.

The art of objection handling is firstly about spotting a true objection. If, for example, someone says, "That's more than I expected to pay." That's not an objection, that's a complaint.

Complaints don't need to be handled; they can even be agreed with.

Client: "That's more than I expected to pay."

You: "We hear that a lot."

But if it is an objection, you need the ability to understand what they *really* mean; that's an art and that needs training.

So, let's explore some common objections so you can better handle them when they appear. Because they will appear and if you're not prepared, they can derail a well-oiled sales machine.

1. I CAN'T AFFORD IT

This will likely be the number one excuse you hear when you're looking to sign up a new prospect or trying to sell more to existing clients. But what does this really mean?

The first thing to determine is whether it's true or not. A great way to test that is to give them a hypothetical situation that removes the objection immediately.

SCENARIO 1

Client: I can't afford it.

You: If we could make it affordable, is there any other reason you wouldn't sign up now?

Client: No

You: Cool, well let's have a look at what we can remove from the proposal to bring the price down.

SCENARIO 2

Client: I can't afford it.

You: If we could make it affordable, is there any other reason you wouldn't sign up now?

Client: Well, I would need to run if by my wife first.

You: Cool, and let's say your wife was happy, is there any other reason you wouldn't sign up.

Client: Well to be honest, I'm not sure the accountant you've assigned to us really understands our business. Is there anyone else who has more experience in our sector?

You: So, let me confirm, if we had someone with experience of working with clients just like you and achieving the results you're looking for, you'd be happy and sign up?

Client: Yes

And then boom, with some simple questions, you've got to the real problem. Just by saying "If we could make it affordable", doesn't mean that you're going to discount the price. There are many ways you can make something affordable. But this is just a device to cut to the truth and you can keep this going, layer after layer.

Even by saying "So, if we had someone with experience of working with clients just like you, you'd be happy and sign up?" doesn't mean that you're going to move them to someone else. It might have just highlighted the fact that you failed to communicate this person's experience well enough in the first place.

But let's say, they truly can't afford it, they're not saying they don't want to work with you, they just don't have the cash.

At this point, you have to consider whether you and your marketing have been effective enough in communicating the value.

People rarely have an issue with finding money for something they truly desire. They will happily go into debt for what they want, remember that.

So, if you're confident in your messaging and that they really can't afford what you have, what are your options?

1. You could look to lower the level of certain services. For example, you could switch from monthly management accounts to quarterly management accounts.
2. You could remove certain services and put them on their roadmap for them to consider in the future.
3. You can stagger start dates of services, which is similar to putting services on their roadmap, but with much more structure and a commitment to when they will kick in.
4. You could get them to fulfil certain functions themselves. So rather than you generate invoices for them, they're going to do it.
5. You could sell them training in specific functions for a one-off fee, rather than an ongoing charge. If you're doing this, you must make sure you set the parameters for what 'good' looks like, so they don't impede the delivery of the other services.
6. You could reduce response times and offer your 4-day turnaround support package rather than your 4-hour support package.

These are all methods for making your service offering more affordable, without you having to discount your fees or losing the client. It puts the onus on them to make a decision about what's most important to them.

Ideally, you need a system that enables you to make these adjustments to services, service levels, roadmaps and staggered start dates **whilst you're with the client**, otherwise the backwards and forwards of the discussion will be painful and futile.

Don't forget, all you're trying to establish is the point where they're happy to start with you. You may have to meet them where they are, with their current financial position and their thinking, to get them to where they need to be. Just never do this by sacrificing your fees.

The reality is, they will still be driving a nice car and have SkyTV. So if they _really_ wanted to afford it, they could sell their car and buy a cheaper one and cancel their SkyTV package. But they won't. They won't make that sacrifice, so why should you? Why should you be the one who suffers?

But you also have one extra trick up your sleeve. As an accounting business, if there's anyone who is able to help them to afford your services, it's you.

So, you could say to them "So, you agree that you need everything I'm presenting here. And you don't want to reduce the service level to lower the price. But you also don't think it's affordable. So why don't we do a one-off, cost reduction exercise. We'll look at what you're currently spending and see where we can help you to make some savings. We'll also review what you're charging your clients, to see if there are any immediate price raises you could make."

You could even charge for this as a one-off, no brainer service.

Getting them to pay a relatively low-cost fee for a short-term project, will help to build further trust in you and in them.

Once they've spent that small amount with you to do this, it will give them greater confidence in the value you can bring and free up the cash to afford your services.

You could even offer a money back guarantee on that project, which says that if you don't uncover savings and additional revenue generating activities that would cover the cost of the fee, within the next 3 months, they get their money back.

If they *really* can't afford your services, help them to afford your services.

2. IT'S TOO EXPENSIVE

If someone says you're too expensive, does it mean that you're too expensive? No, of course it doesn't. It just means that they haven't fully understood the value yet, in exchange for the fee you're charging. You're just going to have to work a little harder to help them to see it.

The problem is that we connect the word 'expensive' to money, and therefore think this has something to do with the **price** side of the equation. It doesn't. This has everything to do with the **scope** side of the equation and its perceived value.

When they say, **"You're too expensive"**, I want you to hear **"So far, I haven't seen enough from you, to want to give this amount to you."**

Secondly, don't take it personally or become defensive. It's easy to think that they're implying you're greedy or ripping them off in some way. Don't allow emotions to come into this.

We just need to rebuild the case, only stronger.

If you've used our **GLOSS Method®** to establish their **Goals, Location, Obstacles, Speed and Solution**, go back over it. Confirm the key points and make sure there's nothing you've missed. Did you go deep enough? Did you dare to challenge them? Did you establish the *real* outcomes they're looking for? Have you provided the certainty that you can help them to achieve them? Do they understand why you've positioned the set of services you have? Do they understand the full value of those services?

Once you've been back through that journey, it's now time to dig into your case studies and to share stories of clients who were in a similar situation to them, and how you helped them to achieve similar results.

They may also be unaware of the level of investment they should be making into the finance function of their business. There are various studies on this, and they typically range anywhere between 2-4% of their revenue.

So they may think you're expensive, but it's just that previous firms have allowed them to **underinvest in the finance function of their business** and you won't.

You can show them what you believe a business of their size should be investing into this function. So, if we went for 3%, a business with £500,000 revenue should be investing £15,000 a year into their finance function... at least.

Showing this puts you in a position of authority and can prove to the client that what they thought was expensive, is actually in line with where they need to be.

You need to be confident that you have done the very best to present the full value of your offering. But what if you've not offered enough?

3. I DON'T SEE THE VALUE OF THAT

Closely linked to "That's too expensive." Is "I don't see the value of *that.*"

So picture this, you've presented your client with a good set of services for a good fee and they proclaim that they don't see the value in *that* offering.

Now what **you** heard was that you're too expensive or your fees are too high, or you need to give some services away for free.

But that's not what they said. They just said they don't see the value in **that**. But that doesn't mean to say they wouldn't see the value in something much more.

Let me give you an example.

You call a hotel to take your partner away for the weekend and they say the room is £300 a night. But you don't see the value in that, and you tell them.

Typically, they will then offer you a cheaper room for a lesser experience. But this is your anniversary; you don't want a lesser experience.

But the hotel never found out it was your anniversary. If they had, they could have gone the other way and presented you with their £1,000 for two nights package, where you're greeted at the gate with a horse and cart, given a guided tour of the grounds, you both get a massage, there are flowers in the room and you sit at the chef's table for dinner.

£600 for two nights may have been too much for the first option, where you didn't see the value, but £1,000 wasn't too much for the second option, where you did.

I had this exact same thing with an accountancy firm we were working with, who had a hairdressing client spending £200 a month. They'd gone back and presented additional services to take them up to £250 a month, but they said they didn't see the value in paying the extra fee, so stuck to the original fee.

What they had failed to do, was to unearth all of the client's challenges and to present the very best solution they could.

After we worked with them, they went back with a different attitude and presented a set of services that were £732 a month. The client signed up on the spot and was happy to do so.

This may seem like a big leap to take and reading that, you may feel uncomfortable in presenting such a proposition to a client.

I remember reading a story of a charity who had approached a wealthy philanthropist and asked for a donation of $20,000. The guy said "No."

A year later they spoke to him again and lowered their request to $10,000, and the guy said, "No way."

They therefore concluded that this guy was actually quite tight-fisted and would never make a donation to their cause.

They got speaking to a person who understood selling and serving, and he intervened just before they were about to make a final appeal for $5,000. He said, "Let me speak to him instead."

The charity said, "Good luck."

The guy walked out of that meeting with a cheque for $100,000.

So what had happened? Did he suddenly find more cash? No.

The philanthropist didn't feel that he'd be able to make any significant impact with $20,000, so what was the point. And by donating less, he certainly wasn't going to be able to make a difference. But with $100,000, he could see some real results being achieved. He had certainty that it was worth his investment. But can you see how the charity arrived at the conclusion that money was the issue.

So, going back to the hairdressing client, what happened? They just developed the confidence to push through and get to the level of investment that gave them greater certainty in even better results.

It was like £200 worth of value a month = No.

£250 worth of value = No thank you

£450 worth of value = No way

£732 of value = Where do I sign?

Have you ever read a book called Jonathan Livingston Seagull? It's about a seagull named Jonathan who discovers that he can fly really high, and with practice, he's able to soar down at great speed into the sea and get to greater depths to where all the fish are.

Meanwhile, all the other seagulls are fighting over the scraps of old fish being thrown overboard from the fishing boats.

You have a choice. To fight over the scraps with everyone else or to develop the skills to fly higher, move faster and go deeper than anyone else, and to find the rewards for both you and your clients.

Clients won't necessarily see the value in what you're offering, *unless* you present the **full value** of everything they *really* need from you.

Remember, they don't have to say yes.

Final story to leave you with here. I remember speaking with an accountant - a really nice guy - who had been haggling with a client around fees for years, of just a few hundred pounds a month.

He'd try to push him up and the client would push back.

He then found out that this client had chosen to invest in a business consultant, to help him to look at where he could save money and generate more profits; working on things like forecasts and scenario planning of what would happen if he increased his prices.

All of these things were well within the skillset of the accountant AND what he loved to do. He just never mentioned them because he wrongly thought the client would never pay

The client paid £3,000 a month to this consultant.

By not offering your client **all** that they need, you are not being fair to them or to yourself. They will either go without or find what they need from somewhere else.

Aim high, in fact aim as high as you can. You'll find that it's far less crowded and far more rewarding.

What's stopping you from flying that high? Fear of falling?

"A fall from the third-floor hurts as much as a fall from the hundredth. If I have to fall, may it be from a high place." - Paulo Coelho

4. I DON'T HAVE TIME

Really? They don't have time? Of course they do. This just means that *you* haven't made it a priority for them to give up something else in their life to devote to this.

The time excuse has nothing to do with time availability and everything to do with how they value their time. It's likely they still lack certainty in the outcome you're offering and have therefore concluded it's not worth giving up their time for it.

If they are not confident that this will even work for them, why *would* they give up their time?

My wife didn't have time to fill in the information required to complete her tax return, FOR THE LAST SIX MONTHS!!!

But she found the time this month to spend three hours having her hair done. Why?

Because she knew exactly how she would feel when she walked out of that salon three hours later... like a million dollars.

She had no idea how she would feel when she completed her tax return information.

"I don't have time" is not a time thing. It's about how certain they are, about how they are going to feel about giving up their time and what the rewards will be if they do. It has always been this way and always will be this way.

When the outcome is certain and you've helped the client to see it as a priority, they **will** find the time.

5. I'LL STICK WITH MY CURRENT FIRM A BIT LONGER

When someone exclaims that they want to leave their current situation as it is, for a little longer, it's important to point out three things – what their pain is that they're trying to escape from, how long they've been in that pain and how nothing has changed.

It's then on you to politely point out that they've already tried that - waiting - and it hasn't worked. In fact, it's got worse and the longer they wait, the worse it will get.

They've actually reached out to you because they know that strategy doesn't work and they're ready to make a change.

What they may have forgotten is how long they've been struggling for and what impact that has had on them. They then need to be shown how things will only deteriorate if they continue on that path and how much longer and potentially more expensive it will be to correct in the future. This is not sales psychology, this is just fact.

Waiting changes nothing. Making decisions is what makes the change. Remind them that they've tried the strategy of waiting and it didn't work. So, when would now be a good time to give something else a go?

6. WE CAN DO THIS OURSELVES

I know how annoying this response can be.

You've trained hard in your specific skill. You've had years of experience, delivering it and learning all the pitfalls and mistakes to avoid. You study changing legislation to ensure that what you do remains compliant. You know the problems that would need to be unpicked and the risks that someone would be exposed to if something were to go wrong.

And then you've got THIS guy, sat in front of you saying "Nahhh, it's easy, we'll just do it ourselves thanks."

This is the equivalent of a householder saying to a professional plumber, that they'll just go ahead and plumb in their new bathroom themselves. They've watched a few YouTube videos and have priced everything up from the local hardware store and think they'll save a fortune.

And this is fine.... until they have something unpleasant leaking through their ceiling and they're having to call the plumber back, pay their emergency fee and have the whole bathroom ripped up.

There are a few ways you can handle this situation, but they all start with forgiveness.

You have to forgive the client for thinking it's easy. It's not their fault that they think like that.

The accounting software companies want to sell their software. They do that by making out that their software is so easy to use; it's just a click of a button. And that's fine, you can't blame them for that. They are selling their software and if somebody was skilled *and* if everything was accurate, then they could do that... maybe.

There's also a high likelihood that you've not articulated the intricacies of this service and everything that goes into it. You've probably not mapped out all the stages of how this particular service works, where the client is involved in the process, what the deadlines are for information and what the consequences would be of them not hitting that.

So, they believe it's easy, have been given no reason not to think it's anything other than easy and are looking for ways to save money.

They legitimately believe that they can either do it themselves or get their member of staff to do it. How can you blame them for that?

The way to handle this is not to become defensive, but to agree with them; "Yes you can do it yourself."

This totally disarms the situation.

You must then establish whether it makes *sense* for them to do it themselves and whether or not they have the skills to do it.

You could even consider giving them those skills and selling training in how to do it to *your* standards. But if you do give them responsibility to fulfil a specific part of their finance function, just remember, you're ultimately accountable for the whole function working properly. If it doesn't and you allowed them to do this component, then it's on you.

If you conclude that you **must** deliver this function yourself, then this is how the conversation might go.

So, let's say they've decided to take a bookkeeping function out of the proposal because they believe they can reconcile everything themselves.

"It is possible that you can do this yourself, you are right.

But even though this appears to be a simple task to do, it's actually quite a bit more complicated than the software companies would have you believe.

We have a 20-point checklist that our team uses every single time to ensure that every transaction is correctly coded, that nothing is fraudulent, that everything is compliant to the latest legislation and that you're benefiting from any tax savings you should be getting.

The main things that can go wrong in doing this are X, Y and Z.

And if that were to happen, this is what would have to be done to correct that. [Explain.]

If any of those mistakes were to go unnoticed, the longer that period of time is, the more work it would take to correct that.

Even with our highly skilled bookkeepers and all of their years of experience, they still have to be very diligent in making sure none of these errors are ever made, and if we ever did make them, then it's obviously our responsibility to fix.

If you were to make any of these mistakes, then you'd either need to know how to fix them or you'd have to pay us our correction fee, which starts at X, for the initial exploratory work, regardless of the size of the error.

[If there are any other legitimate, complicating factors, explain those here.]

So with the nature of your business and the large number or transactions going through your accounts, with respect, the chance of mistakes being made by a non-professional is extremely high.

And because this is such an intrinsic part of everything else working, such as you getting your monthly management report on time, I just wouldn't be confident that we could deliver what you needed, to the standards we need to deliver them to, without us doing this piece of work as well."

This is a very strong and compelling argument to put forward. In summary you've...

- Disarmed the situation, making them more likely to listen to you
- Explained that it's more complicated than it appears
- Explained in depth what goes into this service
- Highlighted the benefits you can bring
- Outlined the pitfalls and their consequences
- Extrapolated those mistakes into the future, showing how they worsen over time
- Explained the possible cost consequences of you having to correct those mistakes
- Communicated your uncertainty about them doing this themselves

After having done all of that, you have two options that YOU control, and one trick up your sleeve you can play.

The two options are:

A) **Allow them to do it themselves.** But this is on the expressed understanding that it is completed to your standard. You can even give them your detailed checklist (which they'll never be able to fulfil.) This will be reviewed after 3 months and if it's not working, it will have to be handed back over to you. And if there were any errors that would need to be fixed, this will be the cost of putting that right.

B) **Refuse to work with them in this scenario.** Explain that if they were to do it themselves, you would be able to make no guarantees about the delivery of the overall finance function or the certainty of achieving the outcomes they're looking to achieve. Explain you pride yourselves on delivering results and just wouldn't be confident you could do that in this scenario. So as a result, you would have to suggest they worked with someone else who would be prepared to work this way.

Whichever route you choose, **you're** in control.

Either they can do it, but only if they work to your standards. You must then set and communicate your standards very clearly and explain what will happen if they're not met.

Refuse to work together because it would jeopardise the fulfillment of the overall finance function and risk the outcomes being met.

For certain services where errors could present large risks and possible fines, you could explain how in the very unlikely event of **you** making those mistakes, you're insured against them. But if they were to make those mistakes, they're not.

And the trick up your sleeve, which you can always play, is to explain the same situation in *their* world.

So, if they ARE a plumber for example, it would be to ask how they would feel if a customer of theirs were to insist on connecting the sewerage pipe to the toilet. Would they be prepared to sign off the bathroom and guarantee their work in that scenario?

And moreover, if the inevitable was to start leaking through the ceiling, would they be prepared to come and clear up the mess?

They don't understand your world, but they do understand theirs.

Bottom line. If you're happy to let the client bring parts of the service in-house without you challenging it, be prepared to clear up the shit when it inevitably happens.

So, these are the six common objections. Learn them. Practice them. The more comfortable you and your team are at handling them, the easier you will find it to understand what the client really means and verbalise that to the client.

You need to prioritise these and set time aside for team training. You can even have fun with them.

We've now arrived at the point in the journey where we're ready to give you the strategy to build out your sales system.

Your head should be thoroughly scrambled. Limiting and conflicting beliefs should have been removed. Fear of judgement and rejection should have disappeared, and you should have totally reinterpreted what selling means to you.

You should be excited about the prospect of presenting the greatest value you can to your clients, for high fees and be ready to deflect any objections that may come your way.

Now I know that this isn't the case. This is going to take time to achieve, but at least you've started and further ahead than most.

In fact, I'm willing to say that if you've subscribed to these ideas and you've come this far, you're probably the type of person who wants to know how to put these ideas into practice and make the difference you know you're capable of making.

If you do, that puts you into the top 4% of firms out there; you are the top 20% of the top 20% and ready to build a sales system that will be adopted by your entire team, loved by your clients and very efficient to run. It will position you as the authority in the relationship, allowing you to be highly valued and command much higher fees. The mental groundwork has been done.

Now the final thing we need to do before we lay out the plan for sales success is to decide what we're selling and what we're charging – scope and price.

MINDSET RECAP

I hope you'll agree that this previous section was significant. It is something you will need to return to again and again and each time you do, you'll take something else. We all take different things depending on where we are in our journey, but if I were to sum up some of the key learnings, they would be...

- The root fear you have about selling, comes down to your fear of rejection and fear of being judged.
- The biggest problem your clients face is that they can't decide what to do.
- The No. 1 reason clients won't buy from you is because they don't trust themselves to make a good decision.
- They will never trust themselves to do that until you can give them **certainty in the outcome.**
- Money is rarely ever the issue for why a client won't buy something from you.
- What people say and what they mean are two different things. Your job is to find the underlying truth.
- Selling is your ethical obligation.
- To sell in quantities or of a quality, less than you know your clients need, is to be selfish.
- Selling is helping someone to make a better decision for themselves, faster.
- To get better at selling, you have to stop selling accounting services and instead, start selling certainty.
- You are enough.

Before we get into scoping and pricing, we've just been through a very heavy mindset shifting section together. I want you to take a moment to reflect.

What has been **your** No. 1 learning so far? I would love for you to connect with me and tell me.

Post it on your favorite social platform – LinkedIn, Twitter, Facebook, Instagram – and tag me in. Post a picture of you with the book or of your favorite section. Post a quote or if you dare, post a video.

Above all, reach out and connect. Search for my profile – James Ashford - or scan the QR code to connect...

SCOPE & PRICE

The final thing we need to do before we lay out the overall sales system, is to decide what we're selling (scope) and what we're charging for it (price).

AGREEING YOUR SERVICE SET

Just because you can do something, doesn't mean you have to do something. These were wise words once said to me.

It's easy to get dragged along by what clients want or what you think the next cool service is to offer, but sometimes that's not right. You have to choose the set of services that meet four key criteria.

Before I outline what they are, I want to explain where we slipped up in our firm.

Clients wanted us to pay their suppliers for them, so we offered it as a service. Everything was fine and we thought we were making money out of it. Then two members of staff made two mistakes in quick succession.

One paid a fraudulent invoice and we had to pay the client back out of our own pocket.

One paid an overseas supplier twice and it took us ages to recoup the money.

Those two incidents more than wiped out our profit for that service across all clients, for the previous 12 months and we thought, what's the point?

Just because clients want something, doesn't mean you have to provide that thing. We can do this out of fear because we think they'll leave if we don't do everything for them ourselves. But that's not the case.

We ceased this service and, instead, trained our clients to pay their own suppliers.

You have to weigh up the risks and the rewards when choosing your service selection. One useful concept to aid you in this is Ikigai.

Ikigai is a Japanese concept that means *a reason for being* and is the intersection between four elements:

- What you love
- What you care about
- What the world needs
- What you can get paid for

I can't tell you which services you should provide. All I can say is that compliance isn't dead; it's the most profitable service set we provide. And all services should be able to stand on their own two feet and be profit centres in their own right.

Whether it's payroll, bookkeeping, compliance, advisory or audit services you provide, each and every one has the potential to be hugely valuable, attract high fees and generate good profits.

I can point to many accounting businesses who are doing very well in some or all of these areas.

I know bookkeepers who are absolutely crushing it.

Whatever service selection you choose, don't dismiss something because historically you haven't been able to make money from it. That thought is from your old self, before you read this book.

CHOOSE YOUR PRICE

How should you price your services?

This is the million-dollar question. Because if you fail to price your services profitably and consistently, then everything I've described in this book falls down.

What is the point in making sales if they don't make you any money?

Being profitable is at the core of everything you do, and I rarely meet an accounting business who has this totally locked down... even the big ones.

In our firm, I believe we have this nailed.

It has taken years of refining, but we have a very clear and sophisticated pricing methodology that ensures we don't leave any money on the table, we charge for everything and we don't permit scope creep.

We base our pricing on a range of logical factors such as their annual revenue, number of transactions, the quality of their record keeping, turnaround times, levels of support and frequency of delivery.

But the trick is then to present that complexity as simply, clearly and transparently as possible to your team and your clients.

This approach has allowed us to raise our average monthly fee to £800 at the time of writing this book and is helping to sign new clients of between £1000 - £3000 a month.

The other reason why you MUST be profitable in the way that you price, is that you have to be a profitable firm. If you're not, what chance do you have of helping your clients to be profitable too, which is why they're coming to you in the first place.

This will give you the firm foundations on which to start building your own pricing methodology.

There are many ways to determine your fees, but these are the main two used by a large number of struggling firms out there...

- What are other firms charging? Let's find that out, then charge either slightly more or slightly less than them, depending on what feels **comfortable**.
- What do we think clients will pay, so that sales conversations aren't going to be that **uncomfortable**?

This may be what you thought at the start of this book, but this isn't you now. Both of those are fear-based questions, designed to keep them within their 'comfort zone.'

But do you know what's crazy? The firms using this approach just aren't comfortable. They're in serious pain.

People confuse 'comfort-zones' with 'familiar-zones.' Just because you're *familiar* with doing things a certain way, doesn't mean they make you *comfortable*.

If you want better results for yourself and your business, you have to make better decisions. Decision making is the only power that moves a business forward.

The quality of your decisions comes down to the quality of your questions. If you want to make better decisions, ask better questions.

So, what about asking questions like...

- How much money would we ideally like to make from this service or per client?
- What fee would allow us to do our very best work?
- What would we have to charge in order to deliver the level of value that our clients would be happy to pay for?
- What would we have to charge in order to be able to attract the best staff so that we know all work will be delivered to the highest standards?
- If you're the owner of the firm, you could ask – "How much money do I want to make personally, to have the life that I

want?" Then... "What would we have to charge to enable the business to pay me that amount?"

This approach may make you feel slightly nervous because then you'll have to justify that fee and develop the skills to attract the clients who are willing to pay it.

When Dyson vacuum cleaners first launched, they were twice the price of their competitors and critics thought no-one would ever pay that. But their product was significantly better, and they did a great job of communicating that value.

When the iPhone first came onto the market, it was again, twice the price of competitors phones, and again critics said they were overpriced. The value of the product, and Apple's ability to communicate that, had people queuing around the block. They sold out.

If you have an incredible service that delivers great outcomes, and you can communicate the value of the service and give certainty, then you can charge significantly higher fees than anyone else is charging, and perhaps higher than even you thought was possible.

Is it hard to charge high fees? Yes.

Is it hard to charge low fees? Yes.

Choose your hard.

Set the fees you want to charge in order to generate the profit you want to make, not to be in line with what others are charging.

Set fees that will help you to deliver the level of service your clients will be happy to pay for.

Factor in everything that can go wrong and be mindful of the risks you're exposing yourself to with certain services. Build in contingency.

If it takes you, on average, five phone calls and ten emails to get a client to give you the information you need to complete their tax return, factor that into the price.

If one in fifty payrolls always need amending, factor that in.

Now while you don't want to be taking the *prices* that other firms are charging, you can use their *methodologies*; there's no point in reinventing the wheel if you can take what has been proven, pressure tested and evolving in other firms for years.

Modelling other people's success is one of the fastest ways to make breakthroughs.

Be bold and if it turns out to be wrong, change it.

USE MENU PRICING

Menu pricing is imperative if you are to build a scalable, thriving business.

You must have a clear menu of services whereby you can sit with the client and logically agree to the services they need, how much that will cost and what the exact details of those services are.

This pricing menu needs to be used consistently across your entire team and all clients and if done correctly, will inspire confidence in your prospect, because they will have greater belief in the pricing you're offering.

If they can't see exactly what services cost and they have a hint that these prices aren't set in stone, they will begin to negotiate and won't be happy paying higher than expected prices.

By clearly displaying your services and pricing, you will find that clients will buy more from you, will be happier to pay higher fees and will sign up more quickly.

This menu of pricing should be built on the logical pricing methodologies, whose calculations sit behind the scenes.

Remember, Paul started with his menu of prices, albeit in a clunky excel spreadsheet, but he had a menu governed by pricing formulas, nevertheless.

PRICE ON LOGIC

Accountants and bookkeepers are logical people. So, a logical pricing framework fits with their sensibilities, which gives them confidence when using it. If you want your entire team to adopt the methodology, it has to work for them.

I therefore advocate charging around logical factors such as number of transactions, their annual revenue and number of staff, rather than time.

So let's take bookkeeping as an example.

If you charge an amount for the time it takes you to reconcile my accounts each month, then your profitability is restricted to what is a reasonable hourly rate.

But if you used logical factors, then you're freed-up to generate more profit. As an illustration, if you charged £1 per transaction that you reconcile, you could use bandings and charge to the upper amount in the band.

For example...

- 0 – 49 transactions
- 50 – 74 transactions
- 75 – 99 transactions
- 100 – 124 transactions

Therefore, if you have an average of 85 transactions per month, you would fall into our 75 – 99 transactions band and would be charged at £1 x 99 = £99 per month.

We then multiply this by the **frequency of reconciliation**. If you don't have this factor in there, it's very easy to lose control of the client and of your profits.

You could also charge by:

- Monthly reconciliation x 1
- Weekly reconciliation x 1.5
- Daily reconciliation x 2

If you have an average of 85 transactions per month that you'd like reconciled weekly, you would be charged £1 x 99 x 1.5 = £149 per month.

These prices and multipliers are for illustration purposes only.

You see, with this method, there's no emotion involved and it's possible to pull this data directly from your client's software in real time.

We even developed a whole concept around this called **Data-Driven Pricing.** There is a great piece of software you can use called **Xavier Analytics**. Among other things, it extracts key financial data from the client's accounting software so we can use live information to easily amend fees with regularity and accuracy.

We built an integration with Xavier so that with one click, we can pull through the client's health score, annual revenue, current run-rate, number of monthly sales invoices, purchase invoices, credits notes, journals, bank transactions and number of bank accounts. This makes pricing services that use those metrics as factors, a breeze.

There's no emotion attached to this at all, just logic.

AVOID 3 TIER PRICING

I hear of a lot of accountancy firms offering their clients three tier pricing for their services – gold, silver, bronze. You may use it yourself. You may have bought into the idea that it 'works'.

And I agree, on some level, it 'works'; but there are many levels more where it fails.

Firms are taught that if you present three sets of prices, then the client will choose the higher options through fear of missing out, and therefore conclude that it enables firms to charge more.

This is not fair on the client and not for someone like you. You understand the psychology behind selling and have the ability to stand up to any pricing objection, which this tries to avoid.

You see, fundamentally, the success of your client's business is dependent on the finance function, which you provide.

It's too risky to allow them to decide what they need; they don't know.

If you were having an operation, you wouldn't want the surgeon to ask you how many stitches you wanted. You would hope that they would put in the required amount to prevent you from dying and bill you accordingly.

It's the same with which services your clients need and the level of service they require.

You should have carried out your due diligence with that client to know where they are, where they want to get to and what they need to overcome to get there.

At this point there should only be **one solution** for them, if you are to be fair.

It's not for you to decide what they can afford.

You need to present the right solution that prevents *their business* from dying.

The reason this normally doesn't happen is because the sales process hasn't been thorough, so you don't have the information you need and you don't have a menu of services. It's normally a case of... "So what do **you** want?"

That should never be the case in your firm. It should always be a case of... "So, based on what you've told me and in our expert opinion, this is what you need and what I would want if I were you, knowing what I know."

Also, if you give your clients total choice, you give them control of the relationship and lose ability to deliver the outcome they want. You put their success in their hands, rather than yours.

You play directly into the clients' greatest fear, which is the fear of making the wrong decision. You've forced them to make two decisions – do I want to work with this firm and what services should I go for?

They should only by asking themselves - do I have the trust to work with this firm? What they need should be decided by you.

To my mind this method is outdated, and with respect, lazy. It's lazy because it avoids you putting yourself in the situation of having to justify a fee that is significantly higher than they expected to pay, or indeed wanted to pay.

But if that set of services is what they need and that fee is right, then you should *have to* justify that fee, and with your new mindset, that should not be hard.

DON'T CHARGE ON TIME

If you are still charging by the hour, then you are punishing yourself for being good and preventing yourself from growing. Allow me to elaborate.

The thing your client values above all else is time; theirs and not yours.

Your client only cares that you can deliver value, impact their business, help them to make better decisions about the future and save them time.

If you could reconcile their accounts and send them their management accounts report, three days after month end, is that more valuable or less valuable than another accountancy firm who takes three weeks to complete the same task? (Assuming that the value of the information was the same.) If time was valued, then your answer would be three weeks.

But your answer wasn't three weeks. It was three days.

So, you value speed over time, because you know that if your client can receive something faster, then they can make better decisions about the future, which will save them money and shorten the time it takes for them to become more successful.

So why would you charge based on time?

If you charge based on time, then there is no incentive for you to improve efficiencies with better technology, better systems, better staff, outsourcing, off-shoring or near-shoring. You therefore restrict your own growth and create a lose-lose situation between you and your client.

Also, the only way you can grow is by recruiting more people because you're selling *their* time for money. And the hardest thing you'll ever do in your firm is recruit and keep people. You've now just attached your ability to grow to the most difficult thing you can possibly do, which is why growth stalls.

Now all that said, I appreciate there are projects which may have to be charged on time. This is ok if it's not the norm, but even in many of those cases, time can still be sold in bundles that connect to outcomes achieved, not just time spent.

CHARGE MONTHLY

Charging your clients monthly rather than annually is critical, for several reasons:

1. The client can manage their finances better. Rather than getting hit with a big bill at the end of the year, clients actually prefer to pay monthly because they know where they are with their finances. It's the same way they pay for gym membership, cable and their car.

2. You can manage your finances better. If you know what you have coming in every month, it allows you to make better decisions about how you should grow your own business.

3. It's easier to grow your revenue. Carrying out regular fee reviews allows you to easily add new services and charge more if your client's circumstances have changed. This is almost impossible to manage if you're charging annually. Charging monthly allows you to easily adjust their fee, add on more and crack on.

4. You don't have to chase the client for money. We use GoCardless connected to Xero. So all we have to do is amend the invoice in Xero and the new fee will be automatically taken the very next month. You might not have GoCardless in your country, but you can achieve similar results with Stripe. Your monthly collection method needs to be solid and ideally sit independent to everything else. This gives you the greatest flexibility to switch it out for a different solution if you ever need to or add in more payment solutions for different situations. Be wary about tying your payment mechanism into other fundamental systems of your business, because if it ever needs changing, it will be much more difficult to move away.

5. You get paid faster. If you charge your client once you've completed their annual accounts and it takes you 6 months to complete them, you could be waiting 18 months before you get your cash. Not good. You need to be getting paid from day one.

6. It removes surprising bills and hatred. If you're hitting your client with one-off bills throughout the year, know this...they hate you for it. At MAP, let's say someone starts ringing up for advice or additional support throughout the month, rather than hit them with a one-off bill for it, we have a different tact. We'd take the hit on the first month and then in the following month say "Hey, it looks like you're needing additional support from us, so rather than hit you with large, one-off bills and discouraging you from calling us, we're going to put you on our SOS Support package. This gives you the confidence that you can pick up the phone anytime and talk to us and it's only £X a month. How does that sound?"

7. You can set goals better. If you know your goal is to increase your monthly revenue by two grand a month, it's far easier for you to reach that goal. You can put clear plans in place to sell more to existing clients or bring on new clients. Without this, it's difficult to set goals and therefore nearly impossible to set plans in place to reach them. Without this, you stay stuck where you are.

So, can you see how that small decision to take payments monthly, rather than annually, has such a huge knock-on effect. Get it wrong and you create frustration throughout your firm and keep yourself rooted to the spot.

Get it right and you create win-win-wins for yourself, your clients and your team.

CHARGE FOR EVERYTHING

We charge a lot more than most firms.

This isn't down to the fact that we're particularly more expensive than other accountancy firms, we just charge for everything!!!

If you go and buy a Mercedes car, and you want a push start button instead of a key, you'll pay extra for it.

If you want 21" alloys instead of the 19", you'll pay extra for it.

They won't give you one thing extra without charging you for it. If they gave you *anything* for free, they'd be devaluing the price of every other Mercedes on the road.

Think about it in other scenarios, restaurants for example.

If you go to a restaurant and want a side order of something, you pay extra for it. And rightly so.

So why should it be any different in the way that you charge and sell your services.

If you just went back through your **existing** client base and charged for **everything** you were already doing for them, I would estimate you'd increase your revenue by 20% like that, without having to do anymore work.

JUST START

Know this: Pricing is never solved; it is only ever tuned.

We ideally need a structured approach, which we know is based on best practice to avoid reinventing the wheel, but even if you get that, it won't be perfect and if you wait for it to be perfect, you will be losing valuable, evidence-based improvements.

The best pricing strategies are not found by waiting and looking into the future. They are found by taking action and looking into the past to see what worked.

Take the best bits. Improve the worst bits. Move forward again. Repeat.

Set the fees you want to charge; not what others are charging.

Charge the fees that will help you to deliver the level of service your client will be happy to pay for.

Get them to where you're about 80 – 85% happy and GO.

Once you have a solid, systemised method of pricing, you can then improve them to be 86% correct, then 88% and so on.

Just know they will never get to being 100%.

Setting the initial pricing framework is actually the greatest stumbling block in this entire process, but the key component of the sales system. It's where the entire value is generated for you and the client.

Thankfully, this is one thing we can help you to fast track through GoProposal which I will talk about right at the very end of the book.

We can help you to generate a suite of services and logical pricing framework, using all the methodologies we use in our firm, combined with the smarts and best practices of other leading firms from around the world.

You just need to answer some simple questions about what you would want to charge for three, very standard services. Based on your answers and our unique algorithm, our wizard will generate a full pricing matrix as a starting point for you to then edit and amend and make work for your firm.

It literally takes 5 minutes to complete and you can then export the price list as a pdf for you to discuss as a team and use in GoProposal or whatever other system you want.

You can get started at **www.goproposal.com/signup or scan the QR Code below**

PART III
THE
BLUEPRINT

THE EFFORTLESS SALES SYSTEM

This effortless sales system has been refined through many businesses I've worked with and honed in the trenches of successful, profitable firms, achieving great results today.

It is woven with many hard-won gems that can have a real impact on the way you sell your services, so please look out for them and take all you can from it.

I don't want you to read through this and be overwhelmed by everything you think you need to do. This doesn't have to be built this week. I just want you to recognise each phase of the system and think what would be reasonable for you to implement as your **version one.**

This is something you can come back to again and again as a guide to building the ultimate sales system. So, as you read through, just imagine this was the journey clients were going on in your firm.

The 7 distinct phases of the sales system are:

1. **Initial Interest** – Capture contact details & instill confidence
2. **Discovery Call** – Ensure you're a good fit for each other
3. **Priming Phase** – Get the prospect ready to buy from you
4. **Meeting** – Unlock the full value of the relationship
5. **Proposal** – Articulate that value professionally
6. **Follow Up** – Ensure the client signs up
7. **Sign Up** – Transition the client into your onboarding process

THE SALES PROCESS BLUEPRINT

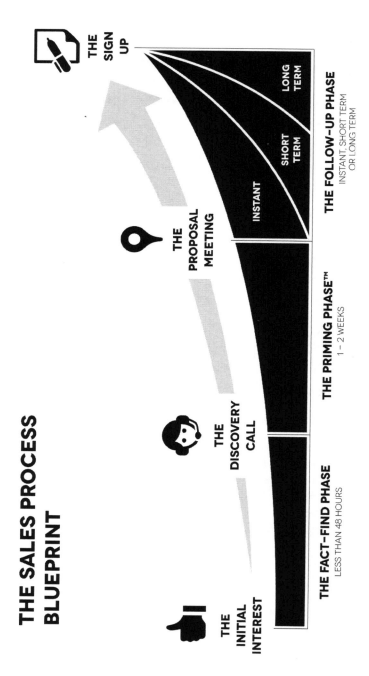

THE INITIAL INTEREST

THE DISCOVERY CALL

THE PROPOSAL MEETING

THE SIGN UP

THE **FACT-FIND PHASE**
LESS THAN 48 HOURS

THE **PRIMING PHASE™**
1 – 2 WEEKS

THE **FOLLOW-UP PHASE**
INSTANT, SHORT TERM OR LONG TERM

INSTANT

SHORT TERM

LONG TERM

If you want to print out the **Sales Process Blueprint** to refer back to, you can get the poster version, print it out, pin up & scribble on. Go to

www.GoProposal.com/blueprint or scan the QR code

1. THE INITIAL INTEREST

When the initial interest comes in, you must, must, must take control. They need to know that they've just discovered **the** expert.

They need to feel your stamp of authority and regardless of how this comes in or who first takes the call or email, you've got to leap straight into action and take control. You've got to wow them because these people are in pain.

Imagine if you went to a hospital with a life-threatening injury and you were greeted with someone who said "Erm...I'm not sure what to do, let me find out."

NO!!!

You need someone who, in their opening sentence, fills you with reassurance that your injury will be treated and your pain removed.

This is where certainty starts to be instilled into the client and it comes down to having a clearly mapped out process, scripting different possibilities and conducting regular training around this with your team.

The goal of this phase is to transition them into what we call the Discovery Call, where we ensure we're a good fit for each other.

So, there are a few different ways in which their initial interest could be shown to you...

THEY'VE EMAILED YOU

If they've emailed you and provided a phone number, you could call them and take them straight into the Discovery Call. Or they've emailed you and haven't provided a phone number, in which case you either need to request it or send them a link to your online appointment scheduling software.

THEY'VE CALLED YOU

If they've called you, then we're straight into the Discovery Call anyway, which is great. If they don't have the time to talk then or you don't, schedule the Discovery Call at that point.

THEY'VE FILLED OUT A FORM

If they've filled out a form on your website (which is quite common) then we take them on a slightly different journey.

1. They complete the simple web form
2. They are then directed to a video explaining that the next thing they need to do is to arrange a Discovery Call with you and what that entails.
3. On that page they are able to book an appointment straight into your Client Coordinator's diary using something like Calendly.
4. They then receive a confirmation email thanking them for arranging the call and outlining what it will involve and what questions you'll be asking them on the call.
5. You then direct them to another short form where they then answer some simple questions ahead of the call. We call this the **fact find phase**. We use this to find out what outcomes they're looking to achieve and the challenges they're facing now. This immediately instills the sense that

we're focused very much on them and will be the right firm to help them achieve their goals. (Every other firm is asking what services they want from them.) You could also dig deeper and ask about the size of their business, number of staff, revenue range, industry etc..

6.   They then receive a confirmation email and text on the morning of the call, reminding them of times and what they can expect on that call.

Now this might seem like a million miles away from where you are now, but with the right systems and the right technology, this is a relatively straightforward process to install.... and not only does it run on autopilot - it WOWS!!!

Imagine that a client is stressed on a Sunday night. They're sitting watching Dragon's Den, thinking about the challenges with their business, and they find you online. They fill out your contact form and are immediately taken to Calendly to schedule a call with you. How relieved will they feel? They will stop their search and feel a huge weight has been lifted, by the very fact that you've enabled them to take a meaningful step closer towards you.

YOU'RE CONTACTING THEM

You may have been handed a referral, in which case you're contacting them.

If you're emailing them, you could direct them to your online booking link.

If you're calling them, you can either take them straight into a Discovery Call if appropriate or use that call to book the Discovery Call.

Whatever happens, they don't get to have a Proposal Meeting without first having a Discovery Call.

Just because you've been given a referral, you're not obligated to give them an hour-long proposal meeting with a senior member of your team. They may be a terrible fit.

This is YOU taking control.

Business is a game, and this is YOUR game... your rules.

If they want to play with you, then they have to play by your rules.

INITIAL INTEREST CHECKLIST

- ☐ **Provide many routes into you** – Make it very easy for clients to get in touch with you.
- ☐ **Respond immediately** – Get back to the client as fast as the technology allows or as fast as is humanly possible. This gives certainty.
- ☐ **Schedule the Discovery Call** – Transition them straight into a Discovery Call via automated appointment setting software and capture any data you need for that call.

2. THE DISCOVERY CALL

The Discovery Call is a 15 - 20 minute call done over the phone or Zoom.

Its purpose is to establish you as the authority, to discover critical pieces of information about them and their business, and if a good fit, to arrange the Proposal Meeting. This would be done by your Client Coordinator or Account Manager.

You need to develop a clear script and then train those members of staff in how to deliver it efficiently. I will give you an example of how this might run.

You also want to capture certain information, which you would need to store in an appropriate CRM system. We use Infusionsoft for this because not only does it store the data, but it also triggers off automated emails, texts, letters and tasks off the back of it. There are also some fantastic practice management systems, which you can use for this such as **Karbon**, **Senta** and **Pixie.**

Now, dependent on how you tackled the Initial Interest and Fact-Find Phase, you may have already captured some or all of this information, which is great. This allows you to confirm the key answers on the call and makes it much more efficient.

So, let's dive into what a call might look like and the questions you need to ask.

You might not use scripts in your business currently. You might think that training your staff in how to follow scripts is too granular. You might be more of a freestyle kind of business than that.

All I can share is my real-world experiences in using scripts, training teams to stick to them and to evolve them and… THEY WORK. They create scalability, consistency, wow and free you up from being involved in the process. They also give you something which can be improved. As with any system, if there is nothing structured there in the first place it can't get any better and will probably be deteriorating.

THE SCRIPT

Let's say James from Acme Limited has booked onto a Discovery call via a web form on your website… and Amy is calling them to deliver the call, this is how the conversation might go.

One important thing to note is that this client might not be a good fit for you, and you will have to tell them that on this call and maybe even why.

The way we handle that is to manage that expectation early on in the conversation, by outlining the potential outcomes of the call.

Hi James,

My name is Amy and I'm the Client Coordinator here at MAP.

Thank you for arranging a Discovery Call with us.

This is an opportunity for us to learn more about your business, understand what's working well, where you're trying to get to, the challenges you're facing and how we can help you to overcome those challenges.

There are three potential outcomes of this call:

A) The first is that we're a good fit for each other and I have everything I need from you to go ahead and book a Proposal Meeting with you.

B) The second is that we're a good fit for each other but I just need to understand more about your business, in which case I'll schedule what we call a Deep Dive Meeting where we can really get under the bonnet of your business.

C) And the third is where I believe we're not a good fit for each other in which case I'll do my very best to make suitable recommendations for you.

Is that ok?

Great. At the end there'll be time for any questions you may have.

Firstly, I want to get a sense of where you are now, so if you do choose to move forwards with a Proposal Meeting, I can arrange that with the person who will be able to best serve you.

A. What prompted you to reach out to us now?

B. What's the main challenge you want us to help you overcome?

C. What's the outcome you're looking for?

D. On a scale of 1-10. How would you rate your current accountancy function?

E. What would make it a 10? (this is an amazing question because it arms you with the precise information you need to convert this prospect into a client)

F.   What is your annual revenue?

G.   How many employees do you have?

H.   What current accounting software do you currently use?

I.   When is your year-end?

J.   What questions can I answer of yours?

[ANSWER QUESTIONS]

Fantastic. So I believe we could certainly help you with those challenges and help you to achieve the outcomes you've described.

The best team member to help you to achieve your goals would be David Arden. David has a lot of experience with helping businesses just like yours, to achieve the goals you've described here.

The next step would be for me to arrange a Proposal Meeting with him if that works with you.

During that meeting we will be taking you through what we call our GLOSS Method® process, which I'll send through ahead of the meeting so you can prepare your answers.

This will enable us to understand how we can best help you and exactly what that would look like from an investment point of view.

We will actually be able to agree to the services and fees together in that meeting and present you with your proposal.

If you're happy with that proposal and you want to proceed, you will be able to sign-up there and then. But there will be absolutely no pressure for you to do so.

In order to make that meeting the best use of your time, there's just one video I'd like to send you to watch BEFORE that meeting.

This outlines how we work and would save us from having to talk about ourselves during the meeting. That way we can focus all of our attention on you and impact your business from the outset.

Does that sound good?

[ARRANGE MEETING]

So I'm now going to send you confirmation of your meeting with a link to the video.

If you have any questions at all, then please call me back.

Thank you and we look forward to meeting with you soon.

This is the type of script you may deliver on your call. You of course need to put it into your own style and so here are just a few pointers...

- You need to avoid being pulled on price during that call, because you really want to be able to establish the value *during* the Proposal Meeting. Your fees may be double what they're currently paying, and if you haven't had a chance to communicate the value of your service to them, you could be losing potential clients. They may ask you what you charge, but they don't really mean that. They nearly always mean 'how do you charge?' The best way to respond is to explain HOW you price, rather than WHAT the price is. So, we would answer with – "Pricing accounting services is complicated, and businesses are complex. We price based on the services you need, the precise service level and logical factors about your business such as the size of your business, number of staff, number of transactions and the quality of your record keeping. The great news is that we are advocates of **clear and transparent pricing**, so we will actually be agreeing all of this together so you will understand exactly what everything costs and how the fee is built up. I *can* tell you that we have a minimum monthly fee of £400 per month."

- We don't allow them to ask questions at the start. This hands control back to them. They can ask their questions at the end…if appropriate. If they are insistent on asking their questions, then I would write them down, acknowledge that you WILL answer them, and then proceed with your call as scripted.

- We ask the *"What would make it a 10?"* question, because this arms you with all the information you need to nail the deal. It also prevents you from talking about things which are irrelevant to the client or which makes you the same as their current accountant.

- We sell them on the idea of watching the video BEFORE the meeting. This is a critical component of the whole process, as you'll see. With some clients, we've even gone to the extent of telling them that if they don't watch the video, then we'd have to rearrange the meeting, as it would be a waste of their time. This is a judgment call but very effective in establishing authority.

- But the principle in play here is that if they're not prepared to watch a 10 or 20 minute video, what chance do you have of them reconciling their accounts or signing up for the package that you're going to want to sell to them.

WHAT IF YOU'RE NOT A GOOD FIT?

What if you decide you're not a good fit for each other and by that, what we really mean is that they're not a good fit for you. Well, this is only awkward if you don't anticipate what those reasons could be, and you haven't formulated a response ahead of the call.

There are three main reasons that we have set responses to. These are:

A) They won't be able to afford our services because their revenue is too low.

B) They only want a very basic service, and we don't offer that.

C) They seem too controlling and will likely be a nightmare.

Revenue too low – "We have a minimum monthly fee of £400 and we advise our clients that they should be investing a minimum of 3% of their annual revenue into the finance function of their business. The level you should be investing would be below our minimum monthly fee and so there are a couple of other firms I could give you the details of, who may be a better fit for where you are now."

Only want a basic service - "We don't just provide a basic accounting service. We aim to provide the full finance function to our clients so they can focus on their core business activities and have the financial insights that will enable them to make better decisions. The service level you're looking for would be below our minimum monthly fee and so there are a couple of other firms I could give you the details of, who may be a better fit for what you want."

Too controlling – (Be respectful of that) "Based on what you've said, I can see you have a very clear way of doing things which is great, but so do we. We have set processes and technology we use that we've evolved and believe to be the best way of doing things. Our systems and team are built around those methodologies and we don't change them on a client-by-client basis. I have great respect for the fact that you've arrived at your conclusions too and so I would advise you need a firm which has a more flexible way of working and can accommodate what you're looking for. There are a couple of other firms I could give you the details of."

This may feel new to you and quite daunting, but you're in control now. You're saying NO to these clients because you're saying YES to being profitable, to serving your other clients to higher levels, to your sanity, to going home on time, to making sure your team is highly valued for what they do and to a hundred other things too.

Remind yourself of what your YES is, and don't worry, there are thousands of other firms out there who will look after them. You're making space for the clients you DO want to work with.

DISCOVERY CALL CHECKLIST
- ☐ **Set Expectations** – Outline what the possible outcomes of the call could be
- ☐ **Gather Key Data** – Take them through your questions to gather key data and to determine a good fit.
- ☐ **Confirm Outcome** – If they're a good fit, book the proposal meeting, if they're not, explain why.

3. THE PRIMING PHASE

THIS is a game changer.

So typically, the Proposal Meeting is arranged and then what happens between that and the meeting... is... NOTHING.

This is a massive waste and creates a huge mountain to climb for the person in the proposal meeting. Wouldn't it be great if you were nearer to the top before that meeting happened?

In our firm, we call this the Priming Phase and we use this time to pre-sell our services before they even turn up to the Proposal Meeting.

If you get this right, it takes none of your time and when they arrive, they will turn up ready to buy from you, rather than to be sold to.

The length of time of the Priming Phase, will determine the amount and type of communication we send out. But for this illustration, let's say it's one week.

THE CONFIRMATION EMAIL

As soon as the Proposal Meeting is arranged, you send them their confirmation email. This is to thank them for booking the Proposal Meeting and to quickly outline what to expect during that meeting.

You then need to reiterate the importance of watching the next video, which will be sent out tomorrow. This message is only very short, but it starts to train the client to take action off the back of your communications.

THE PRIMING VIDEO

The very next day is when we're going to send out an email that contains the main Priming Video.

But before I outline the content of this video, let me explain where this idea first originated.

Paul (the founder of MAP) was awesome in Proposal Meetings and would nail the deal 9 times out of 10. But this created a few problems. In every meeting, he would be going through the same points. This is inefficient and was actually taking up several hours of his time each month.

Not only was this inefficient for Paul, but it was also inefficient for the prospect, because 10 or 20 minutes of that meeting was being taken up with information, which although important, was not terribly valuable to the prospect.

Also, if Paul was to scale his business and to focus on the areas, which needed his attention, he couldn't be involved in every Proposal Meeting. We needed to better leverage the team.

So, we developed this idea of filming Paul, going through all of the amazing points he makes in those Proposal Meetings. We filmed it once and embedded it into an automated email sequence which goes out to the prospect once their Proposal Meeting is booked.

By doing the above, this has...

- Massively freed up Paul's time to be working on his business rather than in it.
- Allowed his team to attend the Proposal Meetings instead of him.
- Primed the client before they even turned up to the Proposal Meeting and pre-sold them.
- Freed up time in the meeting, which the team member could use to give more value to the prospect and to actually invest in the relationship before any money has changed hands.
- Increased our average proposal value from £250/month to £800/month
- Produced a scalable process that has increased the value of his business if he ever came to sell it.

We automate these processes, as it also allows us to 'set and forget' and also track whether they've watched the video or not.

If you know that they haven't watched the video, you could send a polite email before the meeting saying, "I see you haven't watched the video yet, should we reschedule the meeting?"

This is *really* taking control of the process.

It can be politely sold to the prospect on the premise that the meeting would be a waste of their time as you won't be able to deliver the most value you possibly can to them.

What it really does is indoctrinate that person into playing by your rules...or don't play at all.

This may seem harsh at first, but let it sink in. The theory is sound, and it works.

So, let's get back to the content of this Priming Video.

A great video should...

- Be very conversational and natural.
- Describe your story and why you're so passionate about giving great value to your clients.
- Outline the agenda of the proposal meeting and explain that they will be given a Proposal during that meeting, which they can sign up for there and then if that's right for them to do.
- Encourage them to bring any decision makers to that meeting. We want them turning up to buy from you. We're not going to be pushy in the meeting but if they want to hit go, they should be allowed to...we don't want to have more meetings than necessary.
- Bring in relevant testimonials from other clients in the forms of words on screen, as case studies or even as video snippets, if you want to be that adventurous.

Now all of this might sound like a lot of work, but it doesn't have to be. Also don't forget, you are only doing this **once** so you never have to do it again.

If you are looking for a game changer, then this is it.

If you use the **GLOSS Method®** in the proposal meeting as the backbone of your agenda, then this priming video can simply take them through the stages of GLOSS, so they can prepare more thorough answers ahead of time.

THE FINAL REMINDER

On the day before the meeting, you should then send out a final email reminder.

If they haven't watched the Priming Video yet, this is where you can suggest that the meeting be rescheduled or at least acknowledge the fact that they haven't watched the video yet and suggest that now would be a good time to do it.

This is also another great chance to wow them.

For example, do you send directions to your premises in your confirmation email?

Yes? Nice. But do you send a Directional Video?

No?

A Directional Video is where you produce a short film that shows them exactly where your offices are, how and where to park, how to get into your building, which door to knock on or what buzzer to press.

This amazes prospects and is so easy to do.

You could just do this with your smart phone and top and tail it with an animated logo, which you could buy off **Fiverr.com** for... well a fiver.

Wowing your prospects has never been easier.

In this email, you also want to outline the Proposal Meeting's agenda again, the fact that they'll be getting a proposal and to again encourage them to bring any other decision makers.

PRIMING PHASE CHECKLIST

- ☐ **Confirmation Email** – Sent immediately, confirming details of the meeting and that you're sending the priming video through
- ☐ **Priming Video Email** – Sent the following day, preparing them for exactly what to expect in the meeting and could talk them through the GLOSS Method® questions
- ☐ **Reminder email** – Sent the day before the meeting with a directional video showing how and where they need to turn up

If you want to see an example of the directional video in action, go to **www.goproposal.com/reminder or scan the QR code**

4. THE PROPOSAL MEETING

If you have the correct systems in place, then your team member should now be armed with everything they need to deliver great value to the prospect during that meeting. That prospect should be turning up excited, wowed and primed, ready to buy.

THE MEETING LOCATION

You have to make a judgment call as to where the Proposal Meeting should be held. It could be at your offices, their offices, a neutral location or online.

I personally prefer for them to be held in our offices. This again puts you in control of the process, is a better use of your time and allows you to deliver an incredible experience, which blows their mind.

However, I appreciate that Covid completely changed this and we all had to adapt very quickly. So online meetings are totally viable as well, if done properly and can be a gift for everyone involved.

Once you have the system in place in your business, this frees you up to focus on the overall experience and permits you to do some really exciting things such as...

- Having their name and company logo printed on their parking space.
- Having a TV screen with their name and logo on as they arrive.
- Making sure that everyone in your team knows their name and greets them as they arrive.
- Having a cup with their name printed on it as a gift for them to take away, and for extra bonus points, you can even find out what they like to drink and how they take it beforehand (you can establish this in the Discovery Call.)
- Preparing the meeting space so it looks super professional.

If you choose to use Zoom or the equivalent, then you can do your very best to mimic this process virtually.

With Zoom, for example, you can still tell the client how you'd like them to show up and you can still have their name in lights on your screen when they arrive. If you had their address, you could even send them a physical gift to use in the Zoom meeting, such as a pen and branded notebook.

THE AGENDA

Let's say, for argument's sake, that your meeting is 1 hour long. The first 40 minutes of that meeting should be designed to give value to that prospect.

You should be going over the weaknesses and challenges of their current accounting function and showing them how they could strengthen those weaknesses.

You should be discussing their goals and describing what they would need in place to stand the best chance of achieving them.

You should be discovering the obstacles they face in achieving those goals and proposing how you can help them to overcome them.

If you have an effective, consultative sales framework you use, then great. If you don't have one, use ours. You've heard me mention it several times already.

It's called the GLOSS Method®. This stands for:

Goals – where are they heading?

Location – where are they now?

Obstacles – what's holding them up?

Speed – how fast do they want to go?

Solution – what precise set of services do they need from us to reach their goals and overcome their obstacles at the speed they want to go, based on their current circumstances?

This is the fastest method I know to unlock the full value of that client. If you want the pdf with all the guidance notes and exact questions to ask at each stage, grab it from **www.goproposal.com/gloss**

TWO ROUTES

This brings you to the point in the meeting where you have two options.

A)   You don't have everything you need to make an informed decision about your service offering. You may need more time to look into their accounting software for example, or they may need to provide you with additional information. Don't stress. Schedule a second meeting where you will present the services and fees.

B)   You do have everything you need to agree services and fees straight away. This is the route we will follow here.

AGREEING SERVICES & FEES

All of the work we have done so far in preparing your mindset and building this system, brings us to this one crucial moment. You have arrived at the point where you are now going to **present your clients with the very best set of services, that you would want, if you were them, knowing what you know.**

You are also going to confidently present the cost of those services too. We fully break those costs down, line by line, but you may choose to just give one overall price or a price for each set of services such as bookkeeping or compliance.

The important part of this phase is to **build the service list together,** so the client fully understands how the final cost is arrived at. They need to be brought along on this journey with you rather than you just be presented with a final fee, out of the blue.

The key word is to **agree** on the fees.

If they say it's too expensive, more than they're currently paying or they don't see the value, then you know how to handle those scenarios.

If they state very clearly that they want to work with you, they would like to build up to this full-service offering, but this is just too much of a stretch for where they are now, then meet them where they are.

You have done everything right. They understand the value. They're not saying it's too expensive. They're not asking for a discount. They just feel that there needs to be more certainty in place before they commit to everything, but they're willing to build that certainty with you now.

Effectively, you've asked someone to go out for a dinner date, but they just want to go for a coffee at this stage, in broad daylight.

Fine. This is a long-term relationship we're prepared to invest in and build towards. Meet them where they are.

You can do this with one simple question – "Cool, so what do you want to take out, for now?"

You can then take out those services and add them onto their roadmap for them to consider in the future. This takes all the pressure out of the situation.

We did this once with a client. We presented the full service offering that they needed (our ethical obligation) and it came to around £1,500 a month. This was a huge stretch for them, as they were currently paying £450 a month. So, we removed some services, added them onto their roadmap and agreed at £750 a month. This was where they felt comfortable; this was as far as their certainty would extend.

They signed the proposal and we onboarded them very effectively with our process.

They were so impressed with our process, that it gave them the final piece of certainty they needed and within **one week** of them signing up, they agreed to the full £1,500 a month provision, with no pressure from us.

Have the confidence to present the very best set of services you know they need.

Build up the services and prices together so they know where they've come from.

Agree on fees and be prepared to meet them where they are.

The way you start any relationship is the way you start every relationship. The best types of relationships are built on trust, transparency, certainty and respect for each other.

PROPOSAL MEETING CHECKLIST

- ☐ **Wow them when they arrive** – The moment they turn up to this meeting, whether it's in-person or online, they should be made to feel like they are the most important person in the world.
- ☐ **Use the GLOSS Method® Agenda** – Stick to a clear consultative sales framework that unlocks the full value for the client and you.
- ☐ **Agree the fees together** – If it's right to do so, agree to the fees together and meet the client where they are.

5. THE PROPOSAL

I cannot stress the importance of the proposal enough and the dramatic change in results it can produce, if you get all the intricacies of it right.

What I am about to outline to you here has been a decade in the making, refining, honing and mastering.

And I promise to hold nothing back in sharing with you all that I've learnt about producing world-class proposals. Through this device I will help you to sell more of your most profitable services, for higher fees and with an improved conversion rate.

And I'm also going to share with you the ultimate trick...how to do all of this with no effort, whilst you're sat with the client, so they could potentially sign up there and then.

We're talking grand master, voodoo, ninja proposal production here.

This changes everything and sets you apart from nearly every other accounting business out there.

SPEED

So, you know how it goes.

You've just completed a brilliant meeting and you promise the prospect that you'll have the proposal over to them by the end of the week.

Well that week turns into two and it eventually gets over to them, late and tagged onto an email filled with apologies and excuses.

Not only that... you hated doing it and the reason you hated doing it is because deep down, but you also know that it shouldn't be like this; that it could and should be so much easier.

This delay drags out the whole sales process and can create additional problems.

The prospect left your meeting super psyched and ready to sign up. But between then and the proposal landing on their desk... anything can happen.

They could become distracted.

There could be a disaster at work.

Or worst of all...THEY TALK TO OTHER PEOPLE!!!

If you've followed the rest of the guidance in this section, you should have presented them with a proposition that is significantly more than any other accountant they've seen so far, and definitely more expensive than the accountant they've just left.

If you give them the opportunity to TALK TO OTHER PEOPLE, they can easily be talked out of the solution you've just presented them with, because the people they've talked to, were not privy to your conversation.

You must have the mechanisms to be able to produce a proposal instantly, whilst you're sat in front of the prospect.

You want to do this because...

- You don't want to waste time producing it later.
- You don't want to get in the way of them signing up.
- You don't want to allow anything to scupper your hard work.
- You want to start delivering value to their business straight away.
- You don't want to have to waste time and energy chasing them.
- You're not being fair to them if you make them wait.
- The process so far has turned them into a BUYER, so let them buy.
- You've probably told them during the proposal meeting that you're going to save them time, so you don't want to start by wasting a moment, let alone a week or two.

- They expect to be able to procure your services there and then, so at least meet their expectations.

The other **big** reason you want to produce the proposal straight away, is because you want them to at least agree that this is the correct solution to their problems... whilst they're still with you.

To send the proposal a week or so later is to rely on hope.

It's a fingers-crossed approach.

To ping something over which they've not agreed to, is asking for trouble because they'll either reject it straight away or you'll have to go backwards and forwards getting it agreed, and losing more of your precious time, which you don't have.

If they don't walk out of your meeting with a proposal, then you've got this proposal meeting wrong.

PROPOSAL STRUCTURE

Your proposal is a salesperson that goes back with the client after the meeting is over.

The structure of the proposal is critical if it is to convert the prospect with speed, with ease and with the option to upgrade to a better level of service that could deliver even greater value.

Let me take you through the proposal structure I've successfully used over the last ten years. I've used this structure across a wide range of businesses, but when I introduced it to the accounting industry, it was like it had been designed just for them.

I will quickly outline the structure of the winning proposal.

1. **Front Cover** – Include a large, high quality version of your logo and the company name of the client you've produced this proposal for. They love reading their own name. Then include all the contact details of who produced the proposal and who the proposal is for. This helps both parties to get in touch with each other when they need to.

2. **Contents Page** – They need to be able to see at a glance what the proposal contains and where to find what is most important to them...which is normally the costs.

3. **Introduction** – You need to explain what this proposal is all about and congratulate them for taking a step closer towards improving the accounting and finance function of their business. This doesn't need to be that long. They want to know what this is going to cost. But you need to make a promise as to how their future will be better if they take this step. You can personalise this if you want to with exactly what they're trying to achieve, but this isn't that important if they already feel certainty (it is if they don't.).

4. **Testimonial** – You want to follow up that introduction with a testimonial. The testimonial needs to support the promise you've just made them and provides social proof. If your service helps your clients to make better decisions about the future, your testimonial needs to describe how you've helped that specific client to make better decisions about *their* future. Keep it short and benefit focused. No-one

really cares how nice you are, just that you have the ability to impact their business.

5. **Fees** – You need to provide a crystal-clear list of the services they've opted for and what each of those services costs. You could just give an overall package price but there may be people in their business that want to see a breakdown of costs. The way you present the costs is one of the most important parts of this proposal. A lot of firms hide this section near the back of the proposal, thinking that the client will read everything you've put before it. They won't. Think about it. What would **you** do? You just want to see the costs, right? So, you need to present them early on, and provide the supporting evidence afterwards. I like to call them Investment Costs by the way... because this is an investment.

6. **Goal** – You want to remind them of the reason why they wanted your services in the first place. You need to inspire them to take the action you want. They've just seen your costs. This is going to hurt a little. It should. You now need to remind them of the greater pain they're going to overcome by paying your higher monthly fee. So, it shows them how much this is going to cost and why they should want to pay it.

7. **Next Steps** – You need to make it clear as to what they need to do next. They need to see it step by step and those steps need to be simple and pain free. You need to demonstrate how easy it's going to be to sign up for your services and to move their entire finance function over to

you. This is your call-to-action and gives them greater certainty about what comes next.

8. **Services Explained** – You now need to give a breakdown of the services they have chosen and the benefits those services will bring. It's also where you need to clearly outline the specific parameters of the services they've chosen. So, if they've chosen payroll, how many staff is it for and how frequently will it be done? If it's bookkeeping, how many transactions are you agreeing to reconcile for them each month and how often? This is because there will be several people involved in this client relationship and they all need to understand exactly what's being delivered and what's not.

9. **Roadmap** – You also want to build in upsells into your proposal. You don't want a full list of everything you provide, this is lazy. But you do want to provide them with the next steps they'd need to take to upgrade their level of service with you. Most firms either show nothing or everything. You just need to show the next thing they will need from you and to lay it out on the roadmap ahead. They will need to know the cost of these additional services so they can make a decision to include them or not.

10. **Final Testimonial/Quote** – You now want to sign off the whole proposal with an inspirational quote or testimonial that is going to inspire action.

Here are two quotes which I like to use to prompt action...

"Insanity is doing the same thing and expecting different results"

– Einstein

"If all you ever do, is all you've ever done, then all you'll ever get, is all you've ever had."

– Tony Robbins

QUALITY

If the quality of your service is world-class, then the quality of your proposal has to be world-class too. In fact, every aspect of your service needs to be world-class.

Imagine if you'd walked into a top-class restaurant where you'd heard they served amazing food, and when you walked in, you were greeted with a miserable Maître D'. What would you think?

I know what you'd think...the same as me.

But if you changed that experience and made sure that your first impression was an amazing one, I know what would happen. You'd have a better time, spend more money, stay longer and tell more people about it. This is not complicated, so why should it be any different for accounting businesses?

It isn't.

Every aspect of your service needs to wow... especially your proposal.

If you want a client to spend £1,000 a month with you, then that's £12,000 a year. Over ten years that's £120,000.

If you want to be securing clients who are willing to pay you £120,000, then you have to provide a £120,000 experience as soon as they interact with you and then every step along the way.

ONLINE

The technology you use to produce your proposal needs to be online, not just on your computer.

You're a cloud expert, right? You know the benefits of the cloud so I shouldn't have to sell it to you.

But just in case you need a reminder...

- Any member of your team can access it, at any time.
- It can be used on any device – laptop or tablet.
- It's safer and more secure.
- When you update it in one place, it is instantly updated everywhere else too.
- You live and die by the cloud... therefore live by it. To talk to your new prospect about the wonderful technology of **Xero**, **QuickBooks** or **Receipt Bank** and then to dive straight into Excel to generate a Word doc to produce the proposal, doesn't stack up.

AGREE THE FOLLOW UP

I learnt this very early on when I set up my first business.

Agree when you should follow up with the proposal. What most do is give someone a proposal and then not agree when they should follow up.

You should aim to agree to it in the proposal meeting.

A script I learnt early on is this…

"So how long do you think you'll need to be able to make a decision about this?"

Then whatever they tell you, challenge it by saying…

"Is that realistic? Will that give you enough time to speak to everyone you need to speak to, in order to make a decision?"

The reason you need to challenge them on the date is because you don't want to be badgering them when they're not in a position to make a decision. That will only annoy them.

Agree how long they need and then confirm a time and date.

Then here's the pincer move: Get it booked into both of your diaries there and then.

You can even send them an invite.

Lock it down.

This is not being pushy. This is getting you in a position to be able to deliver the value you've promised, because until you get them to sign on the dotted line, no value has exchanged.

If you're not prepared to put in this level of effort to get them to sign up for your services, then I'm going to say you're not being fair to them, in fact, you're being selfish.

If you believe that you can genuinely deliver the value you're promising, positively impact their business, save them tax, save them time, improve their profits and genuinely change their lives for the better, then not to put in the effort to get them to sign, is to be unfair to them.

It's unfair because they're either going to go without your services or they're going to get them from someone else, who won't be as good as you.

It is your ethical obligation to sell them the services they need in the quality and quantities you have proposed and to get them to sign up.

It's that simple.

But there IS a specific way to follow up that is not pushy and continues to give value.

PROPOSAL CHECKLIST

- ☐ **Produce it instantly** – Speed is essential. They need to be given the proposal during the meeting or you've wasted their time, and yours.
- ☐ **Make it professional** – If you provide a world-class service, this needs to be reflected in a world-class proposal.

☐ **Use cloud technology** – You're a cloud expert, so you cannot use desktop software to communicate the value of what you do.

6. THE FOLLOW UP

The follow up is where most businesses lose and especially accounting businesses.

The reason being is that...

- It takes time
- No-one has ever shown you how to follow-up properly
- The client's expectations haven't been properly managed
- We don't know how long to do it for
- We don't know what messages to communicate

So, follow-up is key, and there are some distinct phases to the follow up process.

AUTOMATION

Firstly, it's important to recognise that this process can be automated. This means you can create it once and it will run forever more.

Depending on which system you use, would determine how 'automated' it is. Infusionsoft, Karbon, Senta or Pixie can all handle follow-up tasks and send automated emails to the client, which run on set days and for a specific period of time.

If done properly, the messages can appear very personalised and the whole process will run on autopilot until a specific action happens, such as they sign up or either they or you end the process. We don't need to get into details about this here, but just know that it can all be automated very simply.

I've produced a flow diagram of the Sales & Onboarding systems we have at MAP. It shows how each stage of the journey flows into the next so you can visualize it. If you'd like the PDF outlining all 8 stages of the journey from start to finish, visit **www.goproposal.com/map** and you can download it from there.

IMMEDIATE FOLLOW UP

There are several distinct phases to the follow up process, which you need to stick to so that you have the best chance of influencing the actions that you want and so that you don't annoy anyone.

The phase between the proposal meeting and the agreed follow-up date should be fairly light.

It's to be assumed at this point that they're moving forwards with the proposal and we don't want to appear too pushy or desperate, so we're going to be positive and leave them with space.

The first email should be sent during the Proposal Meeting itself and should contain the Proposal and Engagement Letter. This means that they are armed with everything they need to proceed. This should describe the next steps and have a very clear call-to-action. This should be driving them back to a page where they can digitally sign-off and accept your proposal. This email should also confirm the follow up date, which you agreed during the Proposal Meeting.

GEM ALERT

Can you remember me warning you about spotting the gems throughout this book? Well just in case you forgot that, I'm about to share one with you here that we've had tremendous success with.

As previously mentioned, we have automated emails throughout this system with automated videos that also get shared. But this step is a manual one that is a total slam-dunk, drop the mic, deal-making, game-changing move.

Videos are an incredible way to communicate with existing and potential clients. As soon as the proposal is over, I would get your team member who delivered the meeting to produce an instant, personalised video. We would simply do this using something like **Loom™ – www.loom.com**

We would open up the proposal we've just produced for them and talk them through the services they've chosen and why we feel they will benefit them.

The reason for doing this is because they will no doubt forget certain things you told them and will likely be showing it to other people who weren't privy to your conversation.

On top of that, it genuinely wows them.

In this video, the script goes something like:

Hey James, it was great to have met with you today and thank you for inviting us to describe how we can positively impact your business moving forwards.

As discussed, we have a lot of experience of working with businesses like your own, helping them to overcome the challenges you're facing and in reaching the goals you've set for yourself.

[It's at this point where you run through the specifics of their proposal.]

If you or any members of your team have any questions at all, then please call me direct.

*And if you would like to get everything started so that we can begin having the positive impact on your business, then just click the **ACCEPT MY PROPOSAL** button and we'll get the ball rolling and make moving over to us as smooth as possible.*

Again, any questions, please get in touch and I look forward to working with you in the near future.

All the best...

If you sign-up for Loom's pro version, you can even add a button within the video, which takes them through to the acceptance page of the proposal. This is the next-level activity I described at the beginning of this book.

Which other accountants are doing this? Hardly any, but this is the new world.

If a prospect visited three potential firms in one day, you would be the only one who got the proposal to them on the same day and to send up the follow up video. I know who I'd sign up with.

The very best way to give certainty is to demonstrate it.

There is then one final email to send in this process if the client hasn't already signed-up, and this is the reminder email about the follow up call. This email should go out on the day before the call and should outline its purpose.

Keep it very conversational and make it clear that you'll be calling them to answer any questions they may have about moving forwards with the proposal, and to see if they're ready to make a decision.

That's it.

It should also contain another link for them to sign up, so they are armed with everything they need to confirm acceptance of the proposal.

Done properly, they will have already done it before the call.

You are then going to jump onto the call with this prospect, answer their questions and attempt to get them to hit that sign up button whilst you're on the phone, so you can crack straight on with the onboarding them

But if that doesn't happen, then we need to understand why that hasn't happened so we can determine what to do next?

A.   Do they need longer to think about it? If so, no problem, how long?

B.   Do they have any specific objections about moving forwards? If so, what are they? Handle them

C.   Do they need to speak with other people? If so, who?

D.   Have they decided to not proceed with you at this time? If so, why, and is there anything that you could do to help change their mind?

E.   Is it just a definite no? If so, why? Could we have done anything differently to have got you to make a different decision.

If they fall into A, B or C, we need to move them into **short term follow up.**

SHORT TERM FOLLOW UP

If they're still interested, but not ready to push the button just yet, we now need to keep in constant contact with them.

If you don't continue to help them to make the right decision, you're not being fair to them. Just keep helping them to take baby steps forward.

On the call, make sure that you tell them you have a couple of emails that you'll be sharing with them that they will be able to take some real value from, whichever direction they choose to take.

This gives them an opportunity to say no, don't send me any more.

But don't apologise for these emails. They genuinely are designed to continue to give value and provide certainty that the promises you have made them have already been delivered to others.

One of THE most powerful ways of doing this is to provide further proof with a case study from an existing client, confirming how you have delivered similar results for them.

In the case study, you want to be answering these questions, which are so powerful in helping to convert prospects into clients. These questions are:

1. What was life like before we started working with you and how did that make you feel?
2. What results have we helped you to achieve and how do you feel now?

3. What would you say to someone who had been given a proposal from us and were considering signing up for our services?

4. What would you like to thank us for?

Can you see how powerful those questions are?

Ideally, I would like to get these two people to have a coffee together and for the client to convince the prospect to sign up. There's nothing more powerful than that.

But the next best thing is to recreate that scenario through video and to ask the client the questions, that the prospect needs answering.

Most testimonial videos look pretty but are completely useless because the questions they were asked were irrelevant. No one ever thought how the video would be used strategically as part of a sales system.

But can you see how the answers to those questions would perfectly help transition that prospect from where they are now, to taking that next step with you, towards certainty?

This can be done as the written word or better still, as a video, and the video wouldn't have to be fancy. Your iPhone with a decent microphone (I use the Rode Lapel mic) would be perfect.

If, after that, they still don't go ahead and they need even longer to think about it or they're just not ready to proceed at this stage. Do we just forget about them?

No. We NEVER forget about them

We had a client who we diligently followed up with for 12 months and when they signed, they were a £1,500 a month client. That's a lifetime value of £180,000.

So the answer is NO.

We NEVER stop following up.

But how should you follow up???

LONG TERM FOLLOW UP

This is how we follow up with those clients who haven't made a decision yet.

We are now in a position where these prospects have not chosen to proceed with us...YET!

Now most accountants would let these prospects go at this stage, but this is a huge waste. We've not got them this far for it to stop here, so don't let them go.

Keep in touch every fortnight or at the very least, every month... FOREVER!!!

This normally frightens accountancy firms because you've been sent loads of pushy correspondence in the past, which you found annoying, and you don't want to *be that guy.*

But there's a different approach.

CONTINUE TO INVEST

In this approach, we continue to invest in the relationship; we continue to help and to give value.

Just because they haven't chosen to work with you yet, doesn't mean to say that you can't still help them and if this is automated, it takes no effort (other than the initial setup) for it to run forever more.

Therefore, could you produce 12 articles, 12 videos, 12 case studies and/or 12 short reports that could benefit a prospect? Of course you could; or your team certainly could.

If you could do that, then you could easily build a 12-month nurturing sequence. As well as this, you could post gifts to them. I love sending books to prospects as it really shows your values. Spending £50 on books throughout the year is well worth it to land a £500/month client who stays with you for the next ten years.

Another great thing to do would be to invite them to events. In our firm we have a Round Table event for our clients which we run every month, where we bring in guest speakers to inspire and help our attendees. What we also cleverly do is invite potential prospects to those events too.

We are constantly investing in the relationship and giving value before we even get the business.

So that's the first thing…Invest.

The second thing is that as we get closer to their year-end (which we learnt during the Discovery Call) we begin to ramp things up.

In month ten of their year for example, you could be sending them advice about how they could minimise the tax they pay for the following year.

Because you have now given them so much value, you are now in a fair enough position to ask them straight out if they'd like to have another conversation about working together.

You have invested in them. They can see that you deliver on your promise, so now just ask them...

"Hi, hope you're well and that you've had a prosperous year.

I know we had a conversation last year and I just wondered if now was the right time for us to talk about how we can provide the accounting and finance function of your business.

Unless I hear differently, I'll give you a bell in a few days' time to see if this is something you'd like to explore again.

It will also just be great to catch up and find out how things are progressing."

You can now follow this up with a phone call and any additional emails if need be.

There is nothing stopping you from repeating this process year in, year out and it can all be automated.

The key principle I'm employing here, is one which underpins all successful systems, which is...SEAL THE CRACKS.

Without developing this system, you will no doubt be wasting money and time, burning through a list of prospects that may one day choose to work with you. Be fair to the prospects you already have and install the system that invests in them first and gives them the best chance of signing up for your outstanding service.

Throughout all of this automation, you can be calling them, inviting them for lunch, inviting them to your webinar, passing them referrals, finding out how they're getting on… anything!!!

You just need to be front of mind and as soon as they're ready to press the button, you're the first firm they think of.

If you think this is too much, you will lose out to the firm who doesn't.

Play the long game.

Continue to invest.

FOLLOW-UP CHECKLIST

- ☐ **Immediate Follow-Up** – Send a video of the proposal immediately after the proposal meeting. Send an email before the agreed follow-up date and then call them at the agreed date and time.
- ☐ **Short Term Follow-Up** – Send relevant case studies to fill the client with certainty that you can help them to achieve similar results.
- ☐ **Long Term Follow-Up** – Continue to invest in the relationship with valuable content until they die, buy or say goodbye.

7. THE SIGN UP

So here we are, the big moment… the sign up.

This is where they go from prospect to client in one swift move. The important aspect of this stage is to make it easy and to remove any obstacles.

This process ideally needs to:

- Be online so it can be signed anywhere and anytime.
- Be instantly available as soon as the proposal is created because they may want to proceed there and then.
- Capable of completion within 60 seconds.
- Be legally compliant with their signature and a check box that acknowledges that they've read, understood and have agreed with your terms.
- Instantly trigger off the next system in the process, which is the Onboarding System.
- Instantly trigger off the invoicing and payment collection.
- Send them a signed copy of their Engagement Letter.

When I first implemented this system with our firm and automated this exact process, the owner – Paul - stepped back and watched his senior accountants deliver the presentation to businesses that were as big as he had ever signed up himself. They signed up within days.

This was one of the most exciting and encouraging stages in our time working together because he had 4 people at this level now, all ready to sign-up new clients.

This aspect of the system should be relatively easy to implement, but the place where you win is in the transition to the next step.

THE NEXT STEP

So, picture this...

1. Your proposal was produced instantly and sent to the client with a link to the Engagement Letter.
2. They clicked the link and digitally signed the Engagement Letter within seconds and set up their payment.
3. They then received an instant, signed copy of this in their inbox as well as being instantly directed to a web page on your website.
4. On this web page they saw a video of you, welcoming them to your accountancy firm and congratulating them for making such a great decision.
5. You then tell them that in order to move things forward, all we need to do, is to capture some basic information.
6. Then immediately below this video, there was a form for them to fill out (while they're all excited about signing up for your service.)
7. Meanwhile... your Client Coordinator has been sent an instant message to call this new client to welcome them to your business and to tell them what happens next.
8. Also, the invoicing was triggered in your accountancy software, which was sent out automatically.
9. Ideally, workflows would have been triggered to start onboarding that client and delivering your service to them.

So, they've signed-up, been welcomed virtually, given you all the information you need to successfully onboard them, set up their payment, been invoiced, been welcomed in person and wheels have begun to turn to onboard and service that client.

This is the world-class level I'm talking about.

The great news for you is that there is technology that is within easy reach that can allow you to operate at this level, with next to no effort. A lot of accounting businesses attempt to install systems like this, but it ends up crumbling and then they blame the technology. The problem is rarely with technology and nearly always with either their mindset or process in the first place.

Get your mindset strong. Adopt a proven process. Then turn on the technology. If you do this in any other order it won't work.

SIGN-UP CHECKLIST

- ☐ **Enable swift sign-up** – This should have been made available during the proposal meeting.
- ☐ **Capture payment and invoice** – You need to take the client straight into your payment mechanism either at the time of sign up or closely after, triggering the invoice in your accounting software, which needs sending straight away.
- ☐ **Welcome, capture & trigger onboarding** – Immediately take them straight into a welcome video, capture data while they're motivated and trigger your onboarding process in your practice management software.

This is a very thorough and detailed process. It may seem overwhelming at first glance, but this is something you can keep coming back to.

I just really wanted to illustrate what can be possible for you and help you break through any remaining limiting beliefs.

The one factor that is governing the results in your business and your life is your standards.

If you want to get better results, raise your standards.

This process sets the new standard for everything to follow.

The important thing is not how fast you build this or even where you get to with it, it's where and how you start.

IMPLEMENT THE SYSTEM

Ok, so by now you should be fired up and excited about implementing some or all of this system. However, with that also comes an element of overwhelm.

It's like getting to the top of what you think is the mountain, only to look up and realise you've just got to basecamp and Everest is in front of you. The key to implementing this system is in just getting started. It's in progression not perfection.

The best time to take action is while you're still in the zone; while you still feel charged-up and motivated to make the changes you know you want to make.

The word motivation comes from the Latin – motivus, which means 'to move'. You've just got to start.

As a wise man once said, you don't have to be great to start, but you have to start to be great.

So here's my question...

What one small thing could you do today to start building momentum?

Just do what you can with what you have, but the key word here is **do**. Otherwise, this will have been just another book that was good to read, but that has had **no** impact in your life at all.

Make this the book that makes the difference.

TAKE MASSIVE ACTION

Statistics suggest that only 4% of people who attend conferences or read books will actually do anything with what they learn.

The most profitable accounting businesses are without doubt, the ones who take action continually. They are motivated enough to take the initial actions required to get started, which builds the momentum to keep them going.

They are the ones who focus on progress and not perfection because if you wait for perfection, you'll never start.

They are the ones who start and fix things as they go, knowing that whatever they start with, will be better than what they had last week, but not as good as what they will have next week.

In Japanese business, there is an award, which is fiercely competed for every year called the Deming Prize. It's awarded to the company who displays the greatest degree of Kaizen.

Kaizen translates as continual and never-ending improvement.

The philosophy of Kaizen is that if something keeps improving, then over time the results compound and lead to exponential growth. And it was this philosophy that saw war-torn Japanese businesses with no electricity and no running water, emerge as some of the most successful businesses in the world.

There will be accounting businesses who read this and for whom nothing will change. They will take these ideas into meetings and out of them again. These firms will stay stuck where they are while others pass them by, and they'll continue to be frustrated by their "bad" clients and failing to fully serve their best clients.

They will continue to blame the world for their situation and justify the chaos and overwhelm with a raft of thoroughly thought through excuses. But excuses only sound good to those who are making them.

There will also be other firms who just start. They will take action. They will take these strategies and implement them in their next fee review meeting or with their next prospect. They will make mistakes. They may feel embarrassed. But it's only in taking those first steps that they will pass through into the thriving, profitable firm they know they could be. And it's these firms who will serve their clients better, for longer, get paid more and have less frustration.

In the future, we're going to see a greater divide between the firms who 'get it' and those who don't; those who are thinking entrepreneurially, standing shoulder to shoulder with their clients, building profitable businesses themselves and driving forward at pace, versus those who are clinging on to the wreckage of old ways of doing things, charging by the hour and fighting over the scraps.

Remember, you are not running an accountancy firm; you're running a business.

But most accountants don't have a business, they have chaos.

And while you have chaos, you're unable to spend time on what's important and you'll forever be dragged into what's not important.

The chaos ends when you take control of your systems and the system that needs to be watertight and locked in first is your sales system and pricing methodology.

So if now isn't the right time to sort this out, when is?

THE RED PILL

The coming years will prove to be very testing times for businesses within the accounting industry. People thought that cloud software was disruptive, but then Covid hit and we all quickly learned what disruption was all about.

Storms are going to continue to hit and while they will take some businesses with them, they can also be gifts.

They're gifts because they force the progressive among us to build back into the core foundations and to strengthen our position of profitability.

Businesses who are more profitable, have more money and better cashflow have a better chance of surviving and actually thriving. And when the storm settles, they will be the ones still here, ahead, bigger and stronger than ever before, able to serve their clients to even greater levels.

There are only two ways to generate more revenue in your business, which are to…

1. **Get more clients.**
2. **Give more value to the clients you already have.**

There are only two ways to **get more clients,** which are to…

1. Get more leads.
2. Improve your conversion rate.

And there are only three ways to **give more value to the clients you already have**, which are to...

1. Sell more services to them.
2. Increase the frequency of those services.
3. Keep clients for longer.

The only other factor in this equation that affects how much money you actually make, is your profit margin. There are only four ways you can improve that, which are to...

1. Increase your prices.
2. Sell more services with higher margins.
3. Improve your efficiencies.
4. Lower your overheads.

When you aim to improve each of these areas, you start to see exponential growth in your success because the numbers compound.

So to sum up, if you want to build the strongest, most profitable accounting business you can, there are only 9 things you can do; everything else is a cost. The 9 things you need to focus on are, to...

1. *Get more leads.*
2. **Improve your conversation rate.**
3. **Sell more services to clients.**
4. **Increase the frequency of those services.**
5. **Keep clients for longer.**
6. **Increase your prices.**
7. **Sell more services with higher margins.**
8. **Improve your efficiencies.**
9. *Lower your overheads.*

When most businesses think about making more money, they tend to only focus on two things: let's *get more leads* and *lower your overheads.*

That's fine, but it's restrictive, because it only considers 2 out of the 9 multipliers and you can only lower overheads so far, and getting more leads takes time and costs money.

The other **7 multipliers** have the power to unlock the gold you are already sat on... and I can help you with those 7.

Have you ever seen the film 'The Matrix'?

If so, you'll know that Neo (Keanu Reeves) was offered the blue pill, to go back to how everything was before and forget everything he'd learned. Or the red pill, where he'd be given all the answers, he'd been looking for in one hit. The red pill in your case is **GoProposal.**

GoProposal is the pricing, proposal and engagement letter software that enables accountants, bookkeepers & CPA's to price consistently, sell more confidently and minimise risk across the entire firm.

It's the fastest route to achieving everything I've outlined in this book, encapsulating all of the mindsets, philosophies and strategies to immediately restore balance to your scope and price at the very core of your business, and enable you to optimise the value of every client relationship, making you as profitable as you can be.

GoProposal will enable you to...

- Generate a suite of services and logical pricing framework, using all the methodologies we use in our firm, combined with the best practices of other leading firms from around the world via our wizard. It takes 5 minutes and uses the prices **you** want to charge as its start point.

- Remove the guesswork with a systemised approach to pricing, that uses sophisticated calculations and a logic that your entire team will want to use, and your clients will understand.

- Agree on fees with your clients without any awkwardness, instantly in real-time with a clear menu of services that you can work through together.

- Present the full value of your services in a professional proposal that reflects your brand and uses the exact structure, outline in this book, all setup for you.

- Generate fully compliant engagement letters in seconds that can be digitally & securely signed by one or more people.
- Easily roadmap services or stagger start dates to enable you to meet the client where they are and upsell services in the future.
- Join our incredible peer-to-peer community to engage and ask questions.
- Get access to our accredited Selling to Serve academy for you and your team to use.

You get a 30-day free trial. No card details are needed. We will train you and your team via our live kickstart training sessions.

Just like you've seen in the standards I've outlined for you here, we pride ourselves on providing all of our members with world-class levels of customer support, which I'd love you to experience first-hand.

We are relentless in our commitment to help you achieve the outstanding results you need in your firm, so that GoProposal will always be seen as a great investment for you and more than pay for itself.

Cancelling is easy. We never pressure you or even ask anyone to stay if it's not right. And even if it's not, you will still be able to export a PDF of all the pricing that the system has generated for you.

But above ALL of this, GoProposal will help you to end the chaos. It will give you a truly watertight system that will help you to start relationships with authority and confidence, so you can remove the overwhelm, charge for <u>all</u> the hard work you do and command the fees you're really worth.

This is where you create an unshakable foundation on which to build all other systems.

GoProposal isn't just a piece of technology designed to save a bit of time or streamline a process.

GoProposal is a methodology, a philosophy and a community designed to help you to maximise the value of all your client relationships.

If you see yourself as one of the 4%, who is committed to building a business that delivers the most impact it can, in the most meaningful and most profitable ways possible, then get started at **www.goproposal.com/signup or scan the QR Code below**

REMEMBER...

Charging high fees is hard.
Charging low fees is hard.

Agreeing to a discount is hard.
Saying no to discounting is hard.

Doing work for free is hard.
Charging for everything you do is hard.

Allowing clients to do what they want is hard.
Getting clients to do what you need them to, is hard.

Running an accounting business will always be hard.
But you can choose your hard.

It's your choice.
Choose wisely.

WHAT OUR MEMBERS SAY

"GoProposal is the single most important software, philosophy and community in the accounting industry. The sales, business, technology and people advice is immense. It is not one thing; it is everything and the Facebook group plus the Academy provide unlimited value. You cannot put a price on it ironically. The system value is limitless. "

Keith Lesser | Lesser and Co Ltd

"Signing up to GoProposal has been one of my best business investments to date. As a sole practitioner, the support I have received from the community has been absolutely invaluable. There is ALWAYS someone on hand to help and offer advice on any questions that I have.

The software has enabled me to produce professional proposals, charge higher, consistent fee's and the whole process is so slick. New features are constantly being added, many as a result of suggestions from the users, you really are made to feel part of the 'team'. The customer service and support are so personal and world-class!

Having access to the Academy is like having a personal coach on tap. You can dip in and out and revisit sessions as you make constant tweaks to perfecting your processes. It's a game changer, you won't ever look back."

Rachael Prideaux | Figure Fairy

"Some years ago, I listened to a webinar in which James enthusiastically introduced me to GoProposal. I was definitely sold by the benefits I could see that it would bring to my business.

That turned out to be just the start of the journey, since I have had incredible support from GoProposal. The concept of the GLOSS review has focused my questions in client meetings and the fact I am able to pre-plan my prices within the software which means I can press the button and I am confident in the presentation of our services.

Our turnover has increased dramatically since using GoProposal. And the community support has helped me embrace my business and make so many worthwhile decisions."

Eleanor Shakeshaft | Your Business Accountants

"Before using GoProposal, our whole fee quoting process was a shambles. Everything James has mentioned in this book, we were doing, from finger in the air quotes to what a similar client had been quoted. Our "system" needed an overhaul.

We started using GoProposal in January 2020, just before the COVID pandemic and therefore not the best timing. Or so I thought. In the last 12 months we have signed up over 20 new clients through GoProposal, each with a fee of over double our previous average.

Using GoProposal also encouraged us to look at all the systems in our practice and start the overhaul to what is now a much more efficient, automated practice providing a far better service to our clients.

Gillian French | DNA Accountants

"We started our practice in January 2020 and signed up with GoProposal the same month - honestly I can say that it helped us to ensure we did not underprice our services, charge for everything we delivered in the scope and have tough conversations with our clients so our relationship wouldn't be tough. It also increased our operational efficiency by integrating with our other software."

Mark Sweetman | First Accounts

A NOTE FROM THE AUTHOR

I just want to thank you for coming on this journey and allowing me to challenge you in the way that I have.

If you need someone to give you permission to be you, I'm giving it to you right now; I believe in you, you're enough.

You are here to do good in the world and you're capable of so much.

You can have a tremendous impact on the clients you serve, unlock greater wealth for them and give them the gift of time to enjoy it, through the wonderful work that you do.

And you can also do that for yourself too, and you should.

We all want to make more money and have more time so that ultimately, we can have more choices; choices to do more of the things we love, with the people we love, when we want to do them.

But you must first choose that you want it, know why you want it, that you're going to get it no matter what it takes and you're going to start now.

If not you, then who?

If not this way, then how?

If not now, then when?

TWO FAVOURS

Remember to connect with me on your preferred social platforms and share your key takeaways for this book. It's where we can engage with each other and where I can start to share more learnings with you.

And please leave an honest, candid review of this book on Amazon. This really helps other people in a similar position to you, to know what they'll likely get from reading it. This is hugely appreciated.

A THANK YOU

I must thank my good friend Paul Gough for helping me with the mindset section of this book. Paul is an incredible entrepreneur, working with Physiotherapists (PTs) around the world to help them to build extraordinary businesses. If you know any PTs, direct them Paul's way and I promise they will thank you - www.ptprofitacademy.com

MY WHY

Not quite sure what you were looking for back here 😖

But to reward you for being someone who is always looking for more… drop an email to james@goproposal.com and put **"I've Found the Easter Egg"** in the subject.

I will send you a link to the audio version of this book for free, for you to listen to and share with your team.

Never stop looking to be more, do more and give more.